SUPERNATURAL INVESTIGATION

Michael Williams

BOSSINEY BOOKS

First published in 1993 by Bossiney Books, St Teath, Bodmin, Cornwall.

Typeset and printed by Penwell Ltd, Callington, Cornwall.

ISBN 0948158 82 4

ACKNOWLEDGEMENTS
Front cover photography: RAY BISHOP
Front cover design and tinting: MAGGIE GINGER
Other photographs: NEIL CAMPBELL-SHARP; JULIAN DAVEY;
ROB SCOTT
Drawings: FELICITY YOUNG

ANCIENT STONES ... Avebury, a prehistoric site which weaves a spell around the sensitive visitor.

ABOUT THE AUTHOR

– and the book

MICHAEL WILLIAMS, a Cornishman, started full-time publishing in 1975. He and his wife Sonia live in a cottage on the shoulder of a green valley just outside St Teath in North Cornwall.

In addition to publishing and writing, Michael Williams is a keen cricketer and collector of cricket books and autographs. He was the first captain of the Cornish Crusaders Cricket Club and is today President of the Crusaders. He is also a member of Cornwall and Gloucestershire County Cricket Clubs – and a Vice-President of the Cornwall Rugby Football Union. A member of the International League for the Protection of Horses and the RSPCA, he has worked hard for reform in laws relating to animal welfare. In Cornwall he is a Patron of the Broomfield Horse Sanctuary at Penzance.

In 1984 he was elected to The Ghost Club, and remains convinced Cornwall is the most haunted area in all Britain. His contributions to the Bossiney list include Paranormal in the Westcountry *and* Supernatural Search in Cornwall.

Supernatural Investigation *is Bossiney's 213th title. '13 is one of my lucky numbers', he says. In it he investigates a whole range of supernatural subjects. Ghostly music, superstition, time slips and dreams are only some of the subjects covered. He also devotes a substantial chapter to the question 'What is a Ghost?' in which five serious students of the paranormal define the character and nature of ghostly manifestations.*

'On every page of this book there is a story, experience or account which will challenge belief or disbelief.'

MICHAEL WILLIAMS

SUPERNATURAL INVESTIGATION

OURS MAY BE the age of space travel and increasing knowledge but – and it's tantalizing – the more we seem able to control and understand our environment, the more we become aware of strange happenings which elude – even defeat – logical explanation. The expert, thanks to sophisticated technology and scientific progress, can explain much but not all.

'There are more things in heaven and earth, Horatio, Than are dreamt of in your philosophy.'

Shakespeare's ancient words have a curiously modern ring and relevance.

My first supernatural investigation began in 1965, a few minutes before midnight on Midsummer Eve.

In those days – and nights – the serious investigator felt like an explorer on the edge of an unknown country. Over the years a great deal of information and evidence have been gathered together yet a great deal of uncertainty remains. Perhaps the sensational, controversial nature of the subject is part of the problem.

At the outset of our journey we ought to be clear in our minds about that word *supernatural* – it means 'that which is beyond our known laws.'

Anyone who begins to write or even converse about the supernatural, runs into another immediate problem. For a minority of people there is no such thing as 'paranormal phenomena'. These sceptics insist we, who believe in, say, ghosts, have been fooled, tricked and deluded.

I happen to think it is the sceptic who has been fooled, tricked and deluded. I cannot believe all those eye-witnesses in countries

THE UNKNOWN ... Times were when the serious supernatural investigator felt like an explorer on the edge of an unknown country. Even today, after research and investigation by many eminent people, puzzles remain and challenges lie ahead in the thing we call the future.

all over the world have been mistaken – or lied.

Since 1965 I have interviewed or corresponded with more than 500 people on a whole range of supernatural subjects. Just a few have been charlatans – their versions never getting beyond the notebook stage. The vast majority were responsible down-to-earth characters.

Science has become God – to many people anyway – and here lies the root of the cynicism. In our largely uncharted landscape, which we call the supernatural, strange things do happen – and those strange things defy scientific law and understanding. A healer lays hands on a sick child, and she begins to improve. A Romany gives us a blessing, and suddenly our luck changes – for the better. A tarot reader turns a card, and some revelation about our past or

SEEKER ... Sir Arthur Conan Doyle delved deeply into the supernatural. Ghosts and haunted houses, automatic writing and moving tables, mysterious sounds and voices all appealed to him.

our future is stated loudly and clearly. We see a figure ahead of us – solid, as real as you or me – and then it suddenly disappears through a solid wall.

What was it J.D. Bernal said?

'The full area of ignorance is not mapped: we are at present only exploring its fringes.'

Forgetting the cynical minority – or perhaps not forgetting them – the great majority of *thinking* men and women are willing to *consider* the evidence for these hidden forces. That is progress. Times were when those hidden forces would have been dismissed – without any real assessment. I believe this cocktail of change has come about through men and women of mental ability and scientific distinction seriously investigating the paranormal.

The idea that all investigators into the paranormal are odd characters is a complete nonsense.

Take, for example, Sir Arthur Conan Doyle, the creator of Sherlock Holmes. His life was by no means all novel writing – nor was it all seances and exploring the unknown. He started his working life as a doctor and served in the South African war as a medical officer.

Sir Arthur could write in a train or a room full of people. An all-round sportsman, he played cricket, soccer, rugby, hockey, golf and billiards. He scored a century at Lords as a young man and, at the age of seventy, he was driving around Brooklands racing track at 100 miles an hour. He had played cricket with Dr W.G. Grace and sailed in a balloon over the Surrey countryside. He enjoyed cigars and a pipe. He appreciated good wine, especially burgundy, dressed with a certain style and entertained generously at Crowborough where he employed as many as eight servants: hardly the lifestyle of a crank.

Past Presidents of the Society for Psychical Research have included eminent European scientists. Air Chief Marshal Lord Dowding, Sir Julian Huxley and Professor C.E.M. Joad are just three former members of the Ghost Club. Lord Curzon, one-time Viceroy of India, that master of speed on land and water Donald Campbell C.B.E., and Canon John Pearce-Higgins, Vice-Provost of Southwark Cathedral, are another three contrasting characters who have probed the supernatural.

Going through my files, recent interviews or correspondence on the supernatural include a German professor, a social welfare worker, three clergymen, a university student, two young radio journalists training in the Westcountry, a former headmaster, a lecturer from the United States and a retired farm worker.

Exploration is by no means confined to crackpots. Of course, there are crackpots but probably no more than you would find in almost any other area of activity.

The really encouraging thing is the orderly, more scientific approach to the whole subject.

It is a curious fact that mysteries do not fade away into nothing when the searchlight of science is turned upon them. The more thorough our investigation, the deeper our research, the more certain it becomes that the paranormal phenomena really does happen.

Proof, of course, is a difficult word. In court the judge may accept something as proof; whereas another will dismiss the same evidence with contempt. 'The camera cannot lie' was once accepted as gospel. But today those four words would be ridiculed: there have been too many cases of trick photography. Even a painting signed by the artist is no guarantee. A while back inside my battered old copy of the *Concise Oxford Dictionary* I came across this definition: 'Evidence sufficing or helping to establish a fact'. In pursuing such a complex subject that is perhaps the best we can hope to achieve.

It is the sensational nature of our subject which many of our critics find indigestible.

Early on I was introduced to the sensational nature of the supernatural. The very first poltergeist case I encountered was here in Cornwall, and involved correspondence with the then Bishop of Truro, followed by a lengthy interview with Canon Elias Truscott, the Vicar of St Issey. Had I not been dealing with people of that calibre, I should have wondered whether the accounts were exaggerated.

Inside a house on the Rame Peninsula, during a nightmare week, crockery was propelled and smashed, chairs and tables were lifted by invisible hands and hurled with great force. Canon Truscott, in his own words 'saw the gate-legged table rise squarely with speed and force, stop suddenly at a height of about two feet, and then drop with terrific force.'

As the week unfolded, Canon Truscott believed this psychic bombardment was related to a young boy in the house. In an endeavour to discover whether the boy was playing tricks, the lad had his hands tied behind his back and was sent into the scullery where pots, pans and chairs danced around him.

Ultimately the family doctor was called in – 'something we should have done earlier,' the Canon confessed, 'but you must remember we were up against something none of us had encountered before in our lives.'

The doctor made a thorough examination, pronounced the boy physically fit, and said, mentally, he could neither be certified nor even recommended as a voluntary patient. On hearing the details of the past week, the doctor said nothing they had told him was impossible for the boy. He recalled an instance in a certain hospital, when he had seen a table leave fourteen doctors, sitting at it, and pass through a doorway with only the fraction of an inch to spare.

The doctor advised the removal of the boy from his present environment. He appeared more concerned about the condition of the mother who, in his opinion, was on the verge of a serious breakdown.

On the boy's departure, disturbances at the cottage ceased, and, soon after, the entire family left Rame.

'The remarkable thing about the whole case,' observed Canon Truscott, 'is the violent noise and force with which things were moved ... it still remains to be discovered whether it was a case of possession, magnetism, hypnotism or some force unknown.'

That interview with Canon Truscott took place more than twenty years ago, but only in June 1992 did I hear from two friends – both very reliable characters – of a case in West Cornwall in 1992. Clearly poltergeist activity is not something that has faded away, and interestingly young people were involved in the recent West Cornwall experience.

In these supernatural investigations I have generally concentrated on subjects relating to six areas in which we publish: Cornwall, Devon, Somerset, Avon, Dorset and Wiltshire. But occasionally I have gone beyond those boundaries for the sake of giving a fuller broader picture.

Some years ago I made a fruitless return journey of two hundred miles: a person had telephoned me with some extraordinary claims. But in our face-to-face interview, inconsistencies began to emerge and, there was a gut feeling of being led up some psychic garden path.

On another occasion I interviewed an elderly lady who claimed she was receiving messages from 'out there': automatic writing. She insisted the words were not her own – that she possessed no such vocabulary or writing skill. Once again another set of notes went into the waste paper basket. Yet curiously within a few months a television company interviewed her and the interviewer on film certainly gave the impression he believed her.

In the process of researching this book, Bossiney colleague Sally Dodd asked: 'Do you believe in reincarnation?'

The Hindu and Buddhist belief is that people are reborn in circumstances predetermined by their former lives, and reincarnation will continue until the soul has achieved a state of perfection.

Now though I have interviewed seven people on the subject, I had to say 'I just don't know'. I am not suggesting those seven people were dishonest in any way, but my experience of the field is too limited to give a crystal-clear yes or no.

I mention such cases to underline the fact I'm not gullible. Early years as a journalist give me some kind of mechanism to sense the phoney.

On every page of this book there is a story, experience or account which will challenge belief or disbelief.

Even if half the pages are false or inaccurate, in some way, then the other fifty per cent represent a strong body of evidence. I happen to believe that more likely 90% are genuine. In fact, I have only included accounts where I have believed we are on solid ground. But the sceptic will naturally reach for the salt.

TIME SLIP

THE TERM 'time slip' in the supernatural field means occasions when people have found themselves 'in the past'. In Bossiney territory we find a remarkable example of a 'time slip' in the church at Bradford-on-Avon, Wiltshire.

Back in 1932 an American investigator of psychic phenomena, Eileen Garrett, visited the building with two colleagues. Mrs Garrett went into a form of trance – involuntarily it is said – and for her the scene suddenly transformed. She was no longer in 1932. Against the wall and beside a door, no longer in existence, was a repulsive man. Through a slit Eileen Garrett claimed to see clearly a group of people, all with 'grim and forbidding faces'. Standing in an open yard, they were taking Holy Communion, but not in the usual serene manner of a Communion service. There was a morose air about the whole thing, and, at this point, she was pushed by someone or something – and fell.

Eileen Garrett believed the figure of the character against the wall was that of a priest who felt hostile to his congregation, and the people outside were members of a leper hostel. A niche in the church walls was a common feature enabling lepers to take Communion without entering the church and infecting other worshippers.

The American lady went on to describe the costume of the people outside the church as that of the fifteenth or sixteenth centuries. Rigid segregation imposed by the church authorities did not eradicate leprosy until early in the sixteenth century. Many church people regarded leprosy as a 'divine punishment' and Bradford-on-Avon would almost certainly have had a leper hostel. Why the lepers should look so hostile and why the priest should seem so vicious is something of a Wiltshire mystery. But, assuming Mrs Garrett's identification of the costume was accurate, the phenomenon could have been a time slip to the troubled days of the Reformation when priests and worshippers were often at loggerheads.

Conflict often seems to trigger these slips of time. In neighbouring Somerset, for example, the Battle of Sedgemoor has been re-enacted on a number of occasions – or, at least, fragments of the last battle fought on British soil. Many people, down the years, living near Sedgemoor have accepted in a quite matter-of-fact fashion the sound of hoof beats: Monmouth's men cantering to their slaughter.

Another curious Somerset case concerns the probable ghost of King Henry II. A lady, visiting the Camel villages in the 1920s, was surprised to see a big house standing in a field – she knew the area and had never seen the building before. Not being a local resident, and seeing the house as a very solid construction, she would probably have walked on without giving the matter further thought. However her attention – and interest – were sharpened by the sight of a man and small boy standing 'motionless near the door of the house'. Immediately she was struck by their unusual attire and the fact that they were staring at her. She decided to make a friendly gesture by approaching the house, the man and the boy all vanished. One moment they were they; the next they had gone into thin air.

Further enquiry and investigation revealed that no such building ever existed there, but it is a known historical fact that Prince Henry was sent to Somerset 'for his safety' during the wars between King Stephen and Matilda. The precise location of the house was a closely guarded secret to ensure the Prince's safety. Local folk memory insisted Henry was hidden in this area of the county – and that the lady on her afternoon walk had seen him and his guardian.

There is little doubt about one central fact: the Westcountry has had a remarkable number of time slips.

Why and how do these occur?

Certainly until 1985 I was very unsure. That year I asked Colin Wilson to write the introduction to a Bossiney title *Westcountry Mysteries*, now out of print, and in it he tackled this very subject: 'As absurd as it sounds, I have come to believe that the explanation lies somehow in the earth itself. Let me illustrate my point with a story. Stephen Jenkins is a schoolmaster who lives in Croydon, and who loves to wander round the English countryside with an Ordnance Survey map and a camera. In his book *The Undiscovered Country* he tells of an experience that happened to him at the age of sixteen, near Mount's Bay in Cornwall:

The clumps and bushes were very still in the windless evening light when suddenly I experienced what I took to be a startlingly vivid optical illusion. Scattered among them, motionless but frighteningly distinct, was a crowd, a host of armed men. For a moment I stood stock still, unable to believe my eyes, then I began to run towards them. At once something like a curtain of heated air wavered in front of them briefly – and there were only bushes and stones.

'What he saw was, I think, a kind of optical illusion, but not in the usual sense. Jenkins was probably picking up something that had happened at the place in the past. I have cited many similar cases in my book *Mysteries* – for example how, a year after the battle of Edgehill, locals were disturbed by hearing shouts of men and the noise of cannons. King Charles the First was so intrigued by the story that he sent a commission to investigate it, and these officers, led by Colonel Lewis Krike, presented a report describing how they had witnessed the phantom battle. They seem to have seen something like the phantom army glimpsed by Stephen Jenkins.'

Most of us think of time as the ultimate reality, the inescapable.

Time, like an arrow, *seems* to point in a precise direction: from the past through the present into the future. Sheer commonsense tells us cause precedes effect. Let us take two examples from the sporting scene. Graham Gooch, the England and Essex opening batsman, scores a boundary. Handling his bat with skill, he strikes the ball, and the ball races across the turf to the boundary. It was necessary for Gooch to strike the ball *before* the boundary could be scored. Or let us watch Frank Bruno in the boxing ring, Bruno lands a powerful punch to his opponent's jaw and the man is knocked out – again cause and effect: Bruno's punch came *before* the knock-out.

Yet again and again in my supernatural investigations I get the impression that time can run backwards.

Here is just one example – no, two examples.

When Sonia and I first came to live at Bossiney in the mid 1960s, we often took Tex, our terrier, for walks along the coastline. He loved these excursions – except for one area. He would never venture on to Barras Head, a promontory immediately below the ruins of Tintagel Castle. At one point on this walk, he would stop, then turn back.

We no longer live at Bossiney, but nearly twenty years later I was talking with Felicity Young, a Bossiney illustrator and writer, who lives at Tintagel, about local places and, to my astonishment, she explained how Arthur, her boisterous Welsh Springer Spaniel, undergoes a personality change as they approach Barras Head, confidence suddenly deserting him. Moreover we are not talking of an isolated incident, but regular happenings with each dog on regular walks – and curiously more than a quarter of a century separates the reactions of the two animals.

Clearly both dogs, at different points in time, and independently, were picking up something from the past. Felicity, in her researches for a chapter in *Strange Stories of Cornwall*, discovered a number of suicides had taken place at Barras Head.

It was Professor C.E.M. Joad of BBC Radio 'Brains Trust' fame who once referred to 'the undoubted queerness of time.'

It would therefore be wrong to assume all time slips take us back to a distant past. In 1987 I interviewed Charles Bayfield, then a student living at Trethevy near Tintagel. Not once but twice he had seen ghosts of his living father. On Hallowe'en morning 1990 Tamsin Thomas and I took part in a ghost phone-in at the Truro studios of BBC Radio Cornwall – a live programme – and the majority of our callers had modern or relatively modern ghost stories to tell.

Between what we know and what we do not know – or understand – is a No Man's Land.

GHOSTLY ARMY ... Stephen Jenkins had this sudden vision of a 'host of armed men.'

That young girl standing, waiting impatiently at the bus stop, that old man crossing the road, that young child walking down the

PROFESSOR C.E.M. JOAD ... speaking at a meeting of the Ghost Club at The Savoy Hotel. Picture by permission of Peter Underwood and The Ghost Club.

pavement, carefully avoiding the cracks, that fast modern car which overtook us before we glimpsed it in our driving mirror: we may never see them again.

They could, in fact, be characters from a time slip.

I have often thought of psychometry as a form of time slip. This method of clairvoyance is when the medium or consultant holds a watch or ring or piece of clothing belonging to the man or woman about whom information or forecasts are required. On the occasions I have experimented as the psychometrist I have been surprised by the amount of detailed information coming from the article. Probably psychometry is a combined effort: elements of telepathy and clairvoyance.

My own modest efforts at psychometry and interviews with several seers convince me that impulses reach our brain in a manner which is due neither to hearing nor sight, touch nor taste – not even smell. We call it extra-sensory perception or briefly ESP. I believe we all have this gift to a lesser or greater degree.

The information obtained through psychometry or, put another way, the facts discovered about the past of the owner of the ring or the watch is a form of character reading. Dr Buchanan of the Covington Medical Institute, who invented the word 'psychometry', wrote: 'The past is entombed in the present.'

Dennis Wheatley, who wrote so many novels with occult backgrounds, agreed to be the subject of a television programme. He was smuggled into the studio and during the programme wore a mask which completely concealed his face. An astrologer, John Naylor, a palmist, Miss Jo Sheridan, a clairvoyant, Tom Corbett, and a psychometrist, Douglas Johnson were asked to tell the audience in the studio and the viewers at home all they could about the mystery celebrity guest.

The first three did pretty well, but Mr Wheatley's greatest surprise came last from Douglas Johnson. Dennis Wheatley was in fairly robust health, but for a while had been occasionally – just occasionally – noticing a weakness in his left knee. It happened about only once a week and was so barely perceptible that he had not told his wife about it.

Mr Johnson was handed a pair of braces belonging to Mr Wheatley. He stroked them for about a minute, then said 'There is something wrong with your left leg. You ought to consult your doctor.'

STRANGE EXPERIENCES ... The Rev Frederick William Marshall telling the author about his experiences in two Westcountry churches Poundstock and Gunwalloe: 'More than once at Poundstock I was conscious of someone standing aside to let me go to the altar ...' At Gunwalloe he reflected: 'At service, when I say "The Lord be with thy spirit", I get a response that goes beyond the number of those present.'

But getting back more particularly to time slips – not all of them relate to long ago.

There was the case of the number 19 bus in Plymouth, Devon. Bus conductor Trevor Pearse remembered the details with great clarity. The double decker drew up at a stop on the main road into the city. 'Two ladies, in their thirties, I should imagine, got into the bus followed by two gentlemen. Up the stairs the four of them went. And there was another lady, rather older than the other ones, but as far as I was concerned she was the mother of the two ladies because the three of them looked so much alike. I assumed the men were the husbands.'

ON THE THRESHOLD ... Bossiney author and illustrator Felicity Young, whose dog Arthur has behaved strangely and out of character on coastal walks at Tintagel. Here Felicity is photographed at Gunwalloe Church where the former vicar, pictured opposite, frequently felt an unseen presence.

As the older lady got on to the bus, for some reason she stopped and her face broke into a broad grin. She looked at Trevor Pearse, gave her shoulders a shrug and walked upstairs. Trevor, for his part, saw them as five people simply getting on to his bus. The only thing, which struck him as a little odd, was the that younger people had not been very courteous in letting the old lady get on last.

When Trevor went upstairs to collect the fares, he realized the old lady was no longer on the bus. 'Where's the old lady gone?' he asked. Moreover he proceeded to describe her: 'She was medium build, slightly smaller than medium height – I would have put her at five feet four. She was wearing – believe it or not – a leopard-skin two-piece suit with matching hat and handbag. And she had a diamond or diamond-like butterfly brooch in her lapel. Her hair was greyish, and very well groomed.' He went on to say she was so like these two ladies, she must be their mother.

One of the women told him: 'The woman you've described to us was our mother. The outfit she was wearing was mother's. In fact, we bought it for her. Last time she wore it was when she went out with us. But she died 14 months ago ...'

THE HANDS TURN ... Time seems to point in a precise direction. Yet in my supernatural investigations I get the impression that time can run backwards.

GHOSTLY MUSIC – AND OTHER VOICES

I HAVE never heard ghostly music but then can I be sure? Pip Everard, the Bossiney potter, told me how one weekday afternoon she set out for a walk to St Nectan's Glen near Tintagel.

On the way she was passing the tiny church of St Piran's, when she heard: 'some very beautiful music coming from inside the little building, so beautiful that I stopped to listen. Then the music stopped. That seemed quite natural, so I decided to go inside and have a word with the talented musician.' Pip went inside, but there was nobody there – and nobody had come out through the one and only door.

The Church of St John's, Torquay, Devon has a genuinely haunted reputation. Some say the ghost of Henry Ditton-Newman, who died in the year 1883, played the organ at his own funeral in the church and he continues to reappear. There have been various reports that the building is haunted by the figure of the dead organist and by that of Rector Hitchcock, also dead. Visitors and parishioners claim to have witnessed the Rector's figure near the organ. Others claim to have heard the St John's organ playing without an organist. One theory is this is an incomplete piece of music which Mr Hitchcock was writing just before his death.

Over the years I have had several verbal and written accounts of music coming from empty churches. I suppose it is a natural state of affairs. Music, after all, plays a big part in church life – and indeed in most religions. Moreover it is believed some musicians, who have departed this life, continue to create new music by working through musicians who are alive and well in this world. Rosemary Brown, for example, claims to be used in this supernatural style by distinguished composers like Chopin and Schubert, Lizt and Debussy.

Back in the 1960s I did some feature writing on the arts and sports reporting for *The Guardian*. In January 1966 the newspaper ran an interesting story about a phantom violin in Dorset. Fred Calver, a well-known auctioneer in the town of Poole and owners of the violin, endeavoured to sell it, but there was not a single bid. Maybe the curious history of the instrument deterred would-be buyers.

The previous year the auctioneer's father had died, and was said to have returned several times to play the violin. The instrument, then 78 years old, had incredibly survived the sinking of *The Titanic* in the North Atlantic in 1912. Speaking to a reporter from *The Guardian* Mr Calver said: 'The violin was played by a friend of my father as the ship was sinking. The passengers were singing *Nearer my God to Thee* and he was the only violinist in the ship's orchestra to survive.' But the horrific *Titanic* experience broke the musician's spirit and he gave up playing. I wonder if the phantom violin still exists, and whether it continued to play eerie music. If any readers can update me on this story, I should be very interested to hear from them.

Drumming, I suppose, is a kind of music, and Wiltshire is the beginning or the end of Bossiney publishing territory.

Wiltshire was, in fact, the setting of a truly historic case of poltergeist activity. In a sentence a poltergeist is a spirit who makes a nuisance of himself. This odd Wiltshire story concerns one William Drury, a travelling drummer in the early 1600s, who was apprehended to come before a local JP Mr John Mompesson, who happened to be away from the area at the time. Drury's drum was confiscated and taken to Mompesson Manor. The drummer of Tedworth, now Tidworth, was furious.

When Mr Mompesson returned to his manor house he had a strange reception. He was told violent thumping and drumming sounds had been heard throughout the night. When darkness came again John Mompesson was able to hear for himself. Another drummer's bombardment was underway. The master of the house searched the entire property inside and out, but could find nothing to account for the strange blitz of noise. Gradually the noises diminished to 'a hollow sound'. But as soon as he climbed back into his bed, the mysterious noises started again.

The whole episode, covering a period of two years is well documented and was investigated by one of the pioneers of psychical research, the Rev Joseph Glanvil, who made an important discovery: the violent noises seemed to concentrate on an area around the beds occupied by the Mompesson girls. Subsequent investigations over the centuries have shown young girls are often involved in cases of poltergeist activity. Anyway normality returned to Mompesson Manor after two wearying years – the whole chapter ending as mysteriously as it had begun.

Probably the most legendary 'drum' in the Westcountry is Drake's Drum, preserved at Buckland Abbey. It is believed that the Drum will beat when England is in danger, and is supposed to have been heard before the outbreak of the Great War in 1914, and again in 1939, prior to the Second World War. The theory is that Drake will hear his drum, and return from the grave to save the England he so loved. Early in 1992 doing some research for Tamsin Thomas's second book for Bossiney, I came across some very clear-cut claims about Drake's Drum. Anyone, interested in the subject, should read Tamsin's *Mysteries of the South West.*

There is no doubt some sound phenomena, over the years, has been very impressive. In 1841, for instance, Dr Reid Clanny recorded a poltergeist case – 'Faithful Record of Mary Jobson'. This featured 'exquisite music', heard by many independent witnesses, followed by a voice of 'angelic sweetness' quoting from the scriptures.

In 1987 I came across my one and only case of someone engaging in a conversation with a ghost.

Bossiney colleague photographer Ray Bishop – a man of absolute integrity – told me how, one afternoon in Wadebridge, he was talking with a friend and mentioned he was going to see Mr X, who ran a shop in the town, when his friend told him Mr X had recently died.

Ray therefore postponed his visit to the shop. Instead he called a few days later, and ordered some items from the assistant – an

PIP EVERARD ... who heard ghostly music at Trethevy, was a good neighbour during our Bossiney years. A potter and painter, she had a deep interest in the magical and mystical things of life. Pip gave me an incredibly accurate tarot card reading just two weeks before her sudden death in 1973. Until then I had never understood how the seemingly lucky chance of a fall of cards could signpost the future. She predicted my forthcoming Supernatural in Cornwall *would be a big success – that Sunday evening it was no more than a mass of notes but it went on to sell more than 40,000 copies. During that reading, our last conversation in fact, Pip gave me some very sound advice: 'You're essentially an all-rounder,' she said, 'and in a way that's good, but when you're working on a project you must concentrate on one thing at a time. Enjoy the* **here and now.***'*

order which necessitated the lady disappearing into another area of the building. Suddenly Ray was conscious of Mr X emerging from an office at the back of the shop.

'He looked very solid and real', Ray recalled. 'Though the man's complexion was ashen I quickly realised I had misheard, for though he looked very ill he was clearly very alive. In fact we talked about the weather for the time of year and how it was affecting trade in the town of Wadebridge.

'So when I returned home I phoned my friend and enquired whether I had misheard him about the death of Mr X.

'"No," Ray was told, "he's dead and buried."'

But Ray had no doubt at all: he had both seen and talked with the dead man.

On these investigations I have aimed for facts. However I feel compelled to make some reference to one famous Cornish legend.

The Mermaid of Zennor is one of our great folklore figures.

At this point I had better make a very clear personal statement. I do not believe there can be such a thing as pure legend: no grain of reality. Can there be smoke without fire?

Mermaids appeared in Cornish legends before the arrival of Christianity. Then they were symbols of Aphrodite, the Goddess of Love. Later, with the coming of the Cornish Mystery plays in the Middle Ages, the Mermaid's role changed to portray the two sides of Christ: half-God and half man just as she is half-woman and half-fish.

Here, briefly, is the story. An attractive lady started attending services at Zennor Church. Now though we Cornish have a bush telegraph which could teach MI5 a trick or two, nobody knew anything about her. She was quite simply a mystery. But young Matthew Trewella, the squire's son, a handsome young man with the finest voice in the parish, fell for her. So one Sunday evening, after the service, he followed her down to the cliffs. Neither were seen again.

Years later a ship cast anchor in Pendour Cove, and the Captain suddenly heard a beautiful voice hailing him from the waters. It was a Mermaid with long strands of blonde hair floating around her body, politely asking him to shift anchor as he was blocking the way to her home under the sea, and she wanted to get back to Matthew and their children. A very frightened Captain did just that and hurried ashore with the extraordinary story – seamen always associated Mermaids with bad luck. Anyway the villagers decided to put the Mermaid of Zennor carving in Zennor Church as a warning to young men in future. And she is still there today: a carved figure on a bench end.

Zennor happens to be one of my favourite area of all Cornwall: dramatic moorland running down to the cliffs, facing the vast expanse of the Atlantic. Curiously though, I have read two accounts of the ghostly singing of a man at Zennor – both accounts failed to give precise details like date or the identity of the witness. Is it then a case of mind over matter – wishful thinking?

I put this question to Acora, the Romany clairvoyant, and obtained an astonishing reply.

'One day at Penzance Fair, a woman came to me in a terrible state. She had lost her son. He had gone out one night in a boat with a friend. A perfectly calm sea and a full moon. The friend fell asleep at one stage, and when he woke up the woman's son was nowhere to be seen. He'd vanished into thin air or into the ocean. This happened down in West Cornwall, and, of course, we know the old folk tales of the Lost Land of Lyonesse lying beneath the sea between Land's End and Scilly.

'But as for the Mermaid of Zennor story, I predict not only will the singing be heard loud and clear at a future date, but that the Mermaid herself will be seen – the ghost of the legend!'

Now there is an exciting prediction – and prospect.

Are mermaids figments of our human imagination – or do they really exist? That question has hovered around our coastlines for a long, long, time. On 8 September 1809 *The Times* published a letter from William Munro, in which he described clearly, in detail, a Mermaid seen on the shore at Sandside Bay, Scotland:

'... being a fine warm day in summer, I was induced to extend my walk towards Sandside Head, when my attention was arrested by the appearance of a figure resembling an unclothed human female, sitting on a rock extending into the sea, and apparently in the action of combing its hair, which flowed around its shoulders, and of a light brown colour. The resemblance which the figure bore to its prototype in all its visible parts was so striking, that had not the rock on which it was sitting been dangerous for bathing, I would have been constrained to have regarded it as really a human form, and to an eye unaccustomed to the situation, it most undoubtedly appeared as such. The head was covered with hair of the colour above mentioned and shaded on the crown, the fore-head round, the face plump, the cheeks ruddy, the eyes blue, the mouth and lips of natural form, resembling those of a man; the teeth I could not discover, as the mouth was shut; the breasts and abdomen, the arms and fingers of the size of a full-grown body of the human species, the fingers, from the action in which the hands were employed, did not appear to be webbed, but to this I am not positive. It remained on the rock three or four minutes after I observed it, and was exercised during that period in combing its

LOST LAND '... old folk told tales of the Lost Land of Lyonesse lying beneath the sea.'

hair, which was long and thick and of which it appeared proud, and then dropped into the sea ...'

VITAL ELEMENT ... Water flows under the bridge at Laycock, Wiltshire There is no doubt a high percentage of ghosts do manifest themselves close to water. Springs, underground streams, wells, in addition to rivers and the sea, seem to provide an elemental background that beckons the supernatural.

WHAT IS A GHOST?

WHAT IS a ghost? It's a big question – rather like asking 'What is an animal?' or 'What is history?'

The truth is ghosts are numerous and various. Sightings are as old as recorded history and from all over the world. I believe the evidence for manifestations is so strong the only serious doubt or debate centres on the *nature* of ghosts.

So, at this point in our Supernatural investigation, I decided to put this very question to five people whose opinions I greatly respect.

First, I asked Colin Wilson, the internationally famous author who lives on the south coast of Cornwall. Colin Wilson sprang to fame at the age of twenty-five with the publication of his bestseller *The Outsider* in 1956. Since then he has written, lectured and broadcast for radio and television on a whole range of subjects: novels and plays, and books on philosophy and the occult, crime and sex.

'If you had asked me twenty years ago: "What is a ghost?" I would have replied "A tape recording." I had been convinced by the theories of T.C. Lethbridge – put forward in books like *Ghost and Ghoul* – that strong emotions (such as misery and fear) can be somehow recorded in the place where tragic events have occurred, and can be picked up by people who are sensitive to such things (dowsers, for example). The 'recording medium', Lethbridge thought, is some kind of electrical field, particularly that of water, so ghosts are likely to be seen in damp places, or above underground streams, and so on.

'Even so, I was puzzled when a couple who had seen a ghost of an old man in their Mevagissey cottage said they were quite cer-

COLIN WILSON ... When Colin Wilson's The Outsider *appeared in 1956, it was one of the major publishing events in this century.* The Outsider *was more than a successful book; as a result Colin Wilson became a kind of figurehead for a new generation. Ever since then he has continued to build his reputation with an output of amazing diversity, ranging from the occult to criminology.*

tain that he had seen *them*.

'When investigating poltergeists (for my book of that title) I became finally convinced that poltergeists are spirits of the dead – who can only manifest themselves when a certain kind of vital energy is available – the kind of energy 'leaked' by emotionally disturbed persons. I had already been half-convinced by Guy Playfair, who told me that his researches in Brazil had left him in no doubt that 'spirits' exist (and can be manipulated by 'umbanda' magicians). But when a young girl described to me how she had been dragged upstairs by her throat by a poltergeist, I suddenly felt I knew beyond all doubt that this was *not* some manifestation of her own unconscious mind. (The most popular theory among modern psychical investigators is that a poltergeist is some kind of manifestation of the unconscious mind of a disturbed teenager – 'recurrent spontaneous psychokinesis'.)

'The writing of a book called *Afterlife* later left me convinced that it is impossible to doubt the overwhelming evidence for 'life after death'. All of which leads me to realise that our ancestors, who believed that ghosts were the spirits of the dead ('earthbound' spirits who are often unaware that they are dead), and that witches may be able to make use of such spirits, were probably correct. That does not mean that I now reject Lethbridge's 'tape recording' theory – it applies to what he called 'ghoules' – oddly unpleasant 'feelings' that hang around certain places. But as far as I am concerned, a ghost is a spirit.'

From Colin Wilson to Peter Underwood is to move from Cornwall to Hampshire or the Savage Club in London, from a prolific author to another busy man who combines writing and ghost hunting. His authorship includes *Dictionary of the Supernatural, The Ghost Hunter's Guide, Jack the Ripper, 100 Years of Mystery* and *Exorcism!* – and a great deal more. We at Bossiney are especially indebted to him, for he has contributed eight titles to our list.

Here is Peter's detailed, carefully considered reply to the same question:

'Well, as Professor C.E.M. Joad used to say, "It all depends what you mean" by ghosts. The evidence for ghosts and ghostly activity is formidable, vast and quite incontrovertible. There are literally thousands and thousands of carefully recorded and often independently witnessed experiences from all parts of the world, in all ages and every kind of civilization. The chances of anyone seeing a ghost sometime during their lifetime is reckoned to be as high as one in ten and the various societies and organisations that have been seriously and scientifically recording this subject for well over a hundred years have collected a mass of remarkably good evidence.

'Half a century of practical investigation has convinced me that there are several different kinds of ghosts and personally I am not at all sure that the once generally accepted idea that all ghosts are the spirits of the departed bears much examination. It seems to me that there is overwhelming evidence that on occasions strong emotions can leave behind 'something' that some people might call a ghost.

'This is most often a traumatic experience, a sudden and unexpected calamity or great shock such as sudden death either by accident or by design. Even some animal ghosts come into this catego-

ry. When she lived in Putney Jilly Cooper had to have one of her pet dogs put down and afterwards his ghost used to run around Putney Common. Jilly and her husband just couldn't bear it and it was one of the reasons they moved to Gloucestershire.

'Conversely great happiness, it seems, causes 'something' to linger after death, that might be called a ghost; there are certainly many instances of the ghostly forms of previous occupants being seen in the house or home or garden that they loved; quiet, unobtrusive, gentle phantoms that harm no one. It seems indisputable that we can leave something of ourselves behind and we have all experienced this to a degree. We enter a strange house and think: this is a nice house, a friendly atmosphere, I could live here. In another house we immediately shy away; we don't like the atmosphere, couldn't live there. If we really can leave something of ourselves behind in the place where we live, is it so unlikely that someone, perhaps with a dominant personality, who loves a place almost to distraction, should leave so much of himself or herself behind that after death others see or sense that person?

'There are even ghosts of the living. The forms of people alive and well have been seen by friends and strangers at places miles from where the person is in reality. There is a well-authenticated case in France of a school-mistress who was teaching in a class when 'she' was seen by two other teachers half-a-mile away. As they prepared to greet her, she completely disappeared. Similar experiences had involved her on other occasions. Surely such experiences suggest that in certain circumstances and possibly in certain climatic conditions, the 'ghost' of a living person can be seen – why then cannot the ghost from a once living but now dead person also be seen under suitable conditions?

'It seems to me that the idea that ghosts are invariably the spirits

◀ *INVESTIGATOR ... Peter Underwood, who lives in a small village in Hampshire, has been President of the Ghost Club since 1960. He took part in the first official investigation into a haunting, and has been present at many seances and exorcisms. He has experimented with precognition, hypnotism and clairvoyance. His numerous books on the supernatural have been published abroad and translated into French, Italian and Spanish.*

of the departed runs into difficulty with the overwhelming evidence of the ghost of a person being seen in several different places. A case in point is the ghost of Anne Boleyn, reportedly seen in the house where she may have been born and certainly where she spent happy childhood years, Blickling Hall in Norfolk; Rochford Hall in Essex, where she also lived; the Undercroft at Lambeth Palace where Anne was tried by Archbishop Cranmer on a charge of adultery; the stretch of water by the Water Tower where Anne made her last journey to the Tower; King's Manor, York, where she spent some happy days in her youth; Hampton Court where she lived a few brief years of happiness; Hever Castle where Henry courted her; Sall Church in Norfolk where her heart may be buried; Bollin Hall in Cheshire where she may have been born; Windsor Castle where she appears in the haunted Cloisters; the Tower of London where she met her death and perhaps Marwell Hall in Hampshire too!

'For her 'spirit' to haunt all these places seems unlikely but for 'something' to linger where extreme happiness, distress or whatever was experienced seems more plausible.

'Some of the best-known ghosts are in fact historical figures that apparently haunt so many historical houses and it is an interesting fact that practically all such ghostly figures pass quietly and purposely through the rooms and passages that would have been familiar to them in their lifetime. These figures appear to be solid, they act naturally and are seemingly dressed in the clothes of their time but where structural alterations have taken place they appear to walk through walls and closed doors and if floors and ceilings have been altered the ghosts appear where they would have appeared before such alterations took place and so we have the ghosts at York and Winchester appearing only from the knees upwards because the flooring has been raised or, as at Cambridge, only the head of a person is seen on the floor of a room, the ceiling of a room having been lowered or altered so that where the ghost now walks it interferes with a new floor. Oddly enough when structural alterations are made in a house it not infrequently disturbs the atmosphere or whatever is conducive to ghostly appearances and a ghost may appear in a previously quiet house or a haunted

HAUNTED HOUSE ... Westwood Manor near Bradford-on-Avon, Wiltshire. Mr Denys Sutton, a previous owner, told Peter Underwood the property had at least two ghosts, and that he had no doubts about the haunted bedroom.

house may become unhaunted.

'Other well-documented paranormal activity include cyclic or recurring ghosts; crisis apparitions or death-bed visions (these rarely occur more than four days after the death of the person depicted but they are very common both in times of peace and war); there are haunted objects, especially so-called screaming skulls; poltergeist activity; time-slips; psychic echoes; aerial phenomena and many modern ghosts as well as ancient ones going back to Roman times and earlier: a camp-site in California is haunted by the form of a Neanderthal-like man.

'I have always thought it interesting that children are good ghost-seers: many children do see ghosts and it may be that before our minds become cluttered with civilization we are more open and receptive to these matters. In haunted houses we investigators have often discovered that we will spend hour after hour in serious and complicated investigation with some quite sophisticated equipment and perhaps during the early hours of the morning having experienced nothing of a supernormal character, we dismantle the equipment and sit back for a little relaxation before packing things up – and then disturbances have been reported and it may well be that a relaxed and quiet atmosphere is more receptive and conducive to psychic activity.

'Ghosts, it seems, are concerned with what happened to them, rather than where it happened, although the two often coincide. People who meet premature deaths, be it accident, suicide or murder, often return (if that is the right word) and are seen or heard or felt in the vicinity of the site of the tragedy; and this seems to apply to animals as well as human beings: in California there is a phantom cow, seemingly mourning the loss of its calf, slaughtered by marauders.

'Whether we like it or not there are haunted houses, ancient premises and modern properties; there are haunted hotels, inns, theatres, fire stations, hospitals, airfields, churches and even open spaces. We may not know exactly what ghosts are but that they do exist is beyond argument for anyone who accepts first-hand evidence that would be accepted in a court of law.

'So what are ghosts? Certainly not figments of the imagination for

HEALER ... Barney Camfield of Alphington near Exeter, Devon, is well-known throughout the Westcountry as a healer, lecturer and broadcaster.

how can we explain a distinct and individual figure seen at a particular place by different people on different occasions who have no knowledge that such a figure has been seen there before?

'So what are ghosts? The true answer is we don't know but it seems indisputable that such appearances are seen occasionally by people with healthy minds in healthy bodies. Most ghosts, available evidence would suggest, can be seen by anyone providing that person is in the right frame of mind and in the right place at the right time. And it is always best to be on the safe side: the 16th century Emperor Maximillian of Austria frequently called out his army to ensure in advance of his arrival that there were no ghosts in the houses where he was due to stay!'

Another man who has no doubts about the reality of ghosts is

Barney Camfield of Alphington, Exeter. A well-known healer and broadcaster and minister for many years of the Moretonhampstead Unitarian Church on Dartmoor, Barney Camfield is the author of *Healing, Harmony & Health* and *Loving, Laughing and Living.*

'Ghosts, apparitions, phantoms, spirits are just that,' he says, 'not solidly material. Yet they do, to a degree, manifest in physical form. Either to be seen or heard or to be felt or detected by a human through one or more of the senses.

'The sensitive human receptor is the crucial element. The non-logical, intuitive perception keys in to the emotional (astral) recordings of the past – or the future – because, usually, the time and space can be computed, selected, or "tuned into" by the receptor according to the strength of the emotional or astral waves (vibrations) given off in either the past or the future event picked up by the sensitive person concerned. The sensitive's creative mind then powers up and manifests the physical elements necessary for recognition of the event. He or she then interprets what is experienced. And quite often interprets wrongly – because the limited ideas of the medium, the sensitive, the interpreter, comes into play.

'Among the letters I received on one particular day was one requesting this piece about ghosts and one from a chap I have known for many years. He has on many occasions consulted me about problems connected with his family; primarily two sons whom he had difficulty in coping with during their teenage years after his wife died. She knew she was dying and said, with a smile on her face, just before her demise, that she would keep an eye on them and give them a spot of help if they were ever in desperate situation.

'The letter, about ten foolscap sheets long, brought me up to date and included a somewhat disturbing incident involving his youngest boy who was now twenty two. The lad blamed his father for holding him back and was exceedingly frustrated. I will not go into the details which were included in the letter. The father admits he was probably over protective. The son had reached such a pitch of frustration and anger that he said later he had determined to kill his father. He took a knife from a drawer in the caravan in which he was living and advanced a few steps along the path towards his father's house when he saw his mother appear just a few feet in front of him. He knew she had died and realised that she was an apparition although, as he told his father a short time after, "She looked so real, so solid!" He didn't actually hear any words but knew that she had said, "No! You mustn't do it my darling." He tried to go on but he said that it was just as if she had stood in his way and physically stopped him. He felt her solidity and realised that she had prevented him from carrying out his intended action – just as she had physically restrained him when he was younger and she was alive.

'All the anger and fear left him and he quietly walked in to his father's house and told him exactly what had happened. Dad found it very difficult at first to accept his son's story but I explained that I thought the son had "manifested" his mother – quite unconsciously of course – just when both he and his father had needed "an eye kept on them and also needed a spot of help". The son had remembered this of course and "underneath" knew that he needed help.'

Jack Benney is a fellow Cornishman and keen student of supernatural. We have corresponded on the subject for several years, and I have talked with him about ghosts on two radio programmes.

He was also the subject of a chapter in my book ***Supernatural Search in Cornwall***, so when my mind turned to the question of 'what is a ghost?' I naturally thought of Jack.

Here is Jack's response – as always, thoughtful and wide-ranging.

'I believe there is more than one form of haunting, perhaps because of what may have happened in the past?

'If for example, a person perhaps was murdered, or was killed by accident, or committed suicide under horrifying circumstances, it could leave an imprint or recording on the immediate surroundings, which after a period of time, seem to trigger off a repeat occurrence of that tragedy, for perhaps centuries. These particular hauntings can be very vivid and lifelike and it's only when they fade away from sight you realize that you have seen a ghost.

'Another explanation of how a ghost is seen or materialises is this: Around every human – and this also applies to animals as well, is a life force or inner aura known as the etheric double, an exact repli-

JACK BENNEY … a keen student of the supernatural, by the model of a watermill which he built in the late 1960's in his garden.

ca of that person or animal and when a person is killed, his or her etheric is very strong and shortly after the body dies the etheric leaves the cold body as a cloud, and the exact replica of that person or animal is formed, and afterwards carry out the same habits as its former owner did in his or her lifetime.

'It does not appear solid, as a ghost that materialised from a horrific happening, but more like a transparent apparition, that seems to be able to pass through walls or doors with ease and dissolves at will. Is it, I wonder, the outer garment we all wear, and when we die leaves us for some other plane or dimension?

'Again is it the same etheric aura that leaves the body after a serious heart attack? When for a brief moment the heart stops beating, and a person then may have what is known as a 'out of body experience', when they can leave their body and observe the frantic efforts of the doctors and nurses to start the heart pumping again, and when they succeed the etheric, or spirit, or whatever it is re-enters the living body again. Perhaps after all, they may be two different happenings?

'I have read somewhere that when a ghost is seen wandering around certain buildings or areas, they are either earth bound spirits who have not completed some task on earth, when alive or are reluctant to leave a place they loved. These ghosts are known as earth bound spirits and may haunt a place for centuries.

'Now about poltergeists, those noisy and destructive entities, who centre their attention on the boy or girl about to enter puberty, who have a very strong etheric energy which the poltergeist uses together with his own, to cause great destruction in a household.

'A girl has more etheric energy than a boy and does not need to be in the same room, where crockery etc is thrown about, and broken. The more fear it makes in the family, the more energy is created, and continues perhaps for months or even longer. Only when the boy or girl, is removed from the home does the place become quiet again.

'So what is a ghost?

'I have never heard or read of a ghost having a conversation with a human being, to explain where it came from, or why it comes back to haunt a place. So we may never know for sure how a ghost of a former being of flesh and blood can materialise from something invisible to our eyes to something that seems solid for a short while, then have the ability to become invisible again, and for what reason . . .

'Finally, here is a true account. A friend and her husband were eating pasties on the sands of Perranporth, Cornwall, when they were astounded to see a funeral procession walking sombrely across the sands towards them. There was no road within a mile or more. The only church was the excavated ruins of St Perrans among the sand dunes.

'The cheap crudely made coffin was carried on the shoulders of four men wearing ancient chimney pot tall hats, three of the four women were draped in the widows' weeds that were worn long ago, the six children had buttoned up boots half way up their legs with heavily ribbed stockings. All were present in deepest black.

The funeral procession moved silently past the watching husband and wife, then it vanished into thin air.

'My friend and her husband went into Perranporth and told an old acquaintance what they had see, he was dismayed, "I have known three or four people who have seen that", he said. "And it was always a bad omen."

'My friend's husband was shortly afterwards taken ill and died. He was under 50.'

Ladies usually have the last word, and a lady has the final say in this matter concerning the nature of ghosts.

Lori Reid, a professional hand analyst, is consulted by people from all over the world. Well-known for her television appearances, radio broadcasts and magazine articles, she has a degree in languages and literature.

Venetian, born in Italy, Lori has lived in Britain since the age of five. She is married to a psychologist, and they live in Liskeard, Cornwall, with their two children and two cats.

'Anyone who, like myself, has been brought up in the Roman Catholic religion, will have been acquainted almost from birth with miracles and mysteries, with spirits and ghosts. Resurrections, apparitions and, of course, the Holy Ghost Himself, permeate the teachings of the faith.

'I was taught that everyone has a guardian angel and I imagined a kindly spirit-presence walking behind me or at my side, guiding and protecting me wherever I went. In the bus on the way to school I would make a little space for my 'companion' on the seat beside me. Many were the times when the inevitable over-large lady passenger, spying her chance to accommodate her ample girth on more than her allotted half-share of the seat, would sink her generous proportions down next to me only to discover that, tiny as I was, I would steadfastly resist being shuffled into corner lest (unknown to her) I should squeeze my angel out.

'In my early devotions, I prayed fervently that baby Jesus would appear and come and play with me. I heard about holy statues that would spontaneously shed tears and I knelt for hours in darkened churches scented with incense, staring at the image of the Virgin Mary waiting and hoping that her lovely face would break into a

REPUTATION ... Longleat, Wiltshire, one of the great houses of the region – and one with a haunted reputation. Various people have felt a 'presence' in the Red Library and there have been sightings of a lady in grey. A passage on the top floor of Longleat is known as 'The Grey Lady's Walk'.

smile just for me.

'Perhaps precisely because I was such a devout child, I fancied, when I was four, that I actually did see a vision – I remember clearly waking up in the night and seeing a bright light which burst into all the colours of the rainbow and the most beautiful face I had ever seen appeared through the light and looked down at me.

'I've looked back on that event from time to time and with adult reasoning have thought up all sorts of logical explanations: perhaps it was a dream, perhaps it was my mother who had come to tuck me in, perhaps, perhaps. Yet I know I was awake and my mother then, and still to this day, maintains that on that evening she did not switch on the light ...

'Psychologists tell us that suggestion is a powerful thing, that with positive thinking we can make all sorts of things happen, that our imaginations can manufacture apparitions out of thin air. The children of Lourdes, of Fatima and, more recently, of Medjugorje were all devout believers when they saw their apparitions of the Virgin Mary. People who consequently flock to those holy shrines are, more often than not, also ardent believers, desirous to witness miraculous phenomenon and thus make themselves open to suggestion and become prime subjects for experiencing collective hallucinations.

'So much for religious spirits, but what of more secular ghosts?' What can we make of Ann Boleyn in the White Tower, of Margaret Pomeroy of Berry Pomeroy Castle in Devon, of poltergeists and the thousands of other sightings of ghosts and phantasms and unexplained things that go bump both in the say and night?

'Simply to reject their existence (if indeed existence is the right word!) strikes me as arrogant. Because we cannot explain a phenomenon does not mean we should dismiss it out of hand. Solar eclipses were once thought to be mystical events, harbingers of doom. Now we know differently. Now we can explain these events cosmologically. One day, when our understanding has developed, we will also be able to explain exactly what a ghost is, why some people are more sensitive to sightings than others, how some youngsters are able to trigger powerful poltergeist activity. Perhaps many of these phenomena will be explained as originating from unusual astronomical or meteorological disturbances. But whatever, there is not doubt that one day, just as we are sure to find a cure for the common cold, so we will find a rational explanation for these as yet unexplained mysteries.

'Meanwhile we must still try to make some sense of our world and one explanation for ghostly matters that I favour is that memories somehow become impregnated in the earth, in the stones around us, in the very fabric of our houses. It is as if our thoughts and feelings emit bursts of radiation which seep into the environment and act as a record of the event at that time. Human misery for example, is one such powerful emotion that may become absorbed in this way. Places where brutal or shocking crimes have been committed invariably give off an air of hostility – a menacing, darkly brooding sensation that disturbs one to the core. People who have been to visit the sites of German concentration camps bring back stories of powerful feelings of anguish and suffering that

LOOKING AHEAD … Italian-born Lori Reid, professional hand analyst, in Rocky Valley with the Atlantic Ocean in the distance. She has been described as 'one of the outstanding prophets of our age'.

emanate from such places. They describe an eerie stillness that hangs over the camp, so much so that even the birds are said to avoid flying over.

'Those amongst us who are sensitive to atmosphere, receptive to vibrations, are able not only to pick up these feelings but can sometimes even 'see' the people and events concerned in dematerialised form.

'Other theories concern the nature of time. We think of time as a continuum, a straight line. What if it isn't? What if there are kinks and twists and warps so that the past and the future are interwoven and sometimes at their interstices history, for a split second, meets the present, and people and events come together in some strange way? Mindboggling stuff! Perhaps it is at these intersections that we have the opportunity to glimpse another time, another world. And might we, you and I alive and going about our business, have unknowingly at some point appeared as ghosts to other people going about *their* business in another time, or even in another dimension?

'I asked my two young children if they believed in ghosts. "Yes," they replied emphatically. And what were ghosts, I asked. "Spirits of dead people," they said. "Are they good or are they bad?" I asked. "The nice ones are nice," my daughter told me. "But the bad ones are evil."

'I hope *her* guardian angel will protect her from the evil ones.'

SUPERSTITION

SUPERSTITION is almost as old as the hills. The truth is, superstition goes back to the early first light of Man's history.

Whether it be birth or death, war or peace, love or work, superstition, even in our scientific age, holds a fascination – and power. Peter Underwood in his scholarly *Dictionary of the Supernatural* says:

'Irrational feelings and beliefs that are experienced by the majority of mankind in all civilizations which acknowledge the possibility that ancient beliefs, fears, misinformation and forgetting customs will result in good or bad luck; such superstitions are connected with almost every activity of man, and the superstitious encounter something on which to base an irrational belief in one form or another every day.'

In one short sentence we are looking for luck. The *Collins English Dictionary* has seven references to the word. I like the second and third definitions: '*2. success or good fortune. 3. something considered to bring good luck.*' Luck, of course, is virtually undefinable. If we say that luck is a quality which certain objects possess we are getting somewhere near the heart of the matter. Such objects, we believe, confer luck on their owners, or luck somehow exists in the air around us – sometimes positively helping us, sometimes seemingly avoiding us and sometimes apparently *summoned* to us.

Of course a percentage of people will dismiss luck and superstition as 'nonsense'. They are the same people who sneer cynically about ghosts.

All of which leads us on to omens, the signs that we, the superstitious, claim if such-and-such occurs then so-and-so will happen. To be specific if we find money or a pin on the ground then this indi-

FORGING FORTUNE ... The horseshoe is a favourite among the bringers of good luck, and the old-fashioned blacksmiths, working with fire and iron, were said to have special powers.

cates we shall be lucky. A dog following us home is another favourable omen. In contrast, to stumble at the beginning of a journey or some new enterprise is ominous.

At this point I had better admit I am superstitious. How could I be otherwise? Cornish parents, Cornish grandparents – with Breton and Irish blood back in the family tree. Moreover as someone who is very fond of animals and who campaigns for animal welfare, I have a special interest in the animal involvement in superstition and the supernatural in general. If a rabbit crosses our path in front of us, we are destined for good luck; if the same animal crosses our path behind us, then bad luck is on its way. I was publisher and 'ghost' writer for Acora, the Romany clairvoyant, for several years. He liked seeing a black cat, which he rated lucky, especially if it crossed his path – he'd then put a wish on the cat. But he hated seeing a white cat.

I have a special interest in equine welfare; consequently a horseshoe is never far from me. It is an old favourite among the bringers of good luck. The horseshoe, made of iron, was regarded as an infallible repellent of witches – and witchcraft. The best horseshoes have four nails on one side and three on the other – seven being regarded as the luckiest number of all. The old horse shoes, shaped and made by the old-fashioned blacksmiths, had an extra quality because the blacksmiths, for centuries, were said to have special powers due to their work with fire and iron. Horses themselves have a significant role in the field of magic – having been sacred animals in many cultures, ridden by heroes and gods. There is an ancient country tradition that a horseshoe found on the road is especially lucky, particularly if it has been cast from the near hind leg of a grey mare.

Horse racing remains one of the most popular forms of gambling in the world and many backers have very personal methods for picking winners – or, at least, trying to pick them. Some put faith in a pin, jabbing it at random into the list of runners, believing the traditional virtue of the pin will do the trick. Others back horses whose jockeys wear their 'lucky' colours, and still others back the 'lucky' numbers which the horses carry. Backers will even resort to complex systems of divination by numerology, astrology, or dream interpretation. The serious student of form will predictably dismiss these methods as 'more nonsense', but they, with all their time and effort spent studying form, breeding, jockeys and trainers, race courses and the going, seem to lose as often as the rest of us.

One of racing's most celebrated ghosts is that of Fred Archer who was champion jockey for 13 successive seasons – 1874-86 – who rode five Derby winners and won fifteen other classic races. In all he rode 2,748 winners, his high noon coming in 1885 when he rode 246 winners in the season, a record that remained until 1933 and Sir Gordon Richards. Archer, a hot tempered character who hated his rivals, died at the age of twenty-nine. Some racing people consider his ghost has accounted for bewildering mishaps on the Newmarket course, notably in 1950 when the Aga Khan's horse Kermanshaf fell in a flat race. Charlie Smirke, the jockey, said he saw nothing but the horse stumbled over *something*. The previous season a horse called Excalibur fell at precisely the same spot – a strange coincidence. Maybe not, because jockeys and spectators claim to have seen something white and formless hovering in the air at the height of the horse rider.

Sportsmen are often notoriously superstitious. That great footballer Jackie Charlton always preferred to be the last player to run on to the field. Nobby Stiles, formerly Manchester United, always left his laces undone until he was out on the field of play.

Team games seem to produce special brands of superstition among the players, not only the wearing of amulets but preparation rituals including the habit of wearing the same articles of clothing that had been worn when a winning streak had begun. Some players put on the left sock or left boot before the right, and so on. Even powerful boxers have clung to superstition. The French Georges Carpentier would never fight unless his manager was wearing a ragged old coat which he had had for fifteen years. Our legendary Cornishman Bob Fitzsimmons, who became heavyweight champion of the world always kept a horseshoe nailed up in his training camp. Ezzard Charles once declined to go into the ring until a colleague had retrieved his 'lucky piece' – an old robe which his wife had put in the dustbin!

The magician Aleister Crowley, 'the wickedest man in the world,' was ultra careful to ensure none of his hair or nail parings fell into the hands of rival magicians. He took such precaution because, according to the law of magic, anything that was once part of the body, particularly the head, retains its connection – even when physically separated from the person concerned.

It is an interesting fact that whereas many people, especially children, accept ghosts placidly, almost naturally, animals in stark contrast, often react in severely disturbed fashion. Horses sweat and rear, or sometimes swerve, dogs howl and shiver, milking cows go dry, and cats arch their backs and spit.

We seem to have strayed somewhat from superstition. But have we? There are many angles.

Numbers have long played a significant role in superstition – and the pursuit of good luck. The four-leaved clover, for example, draws its power from the mystical connotations of the number four: a number which is the symbol of balance, unity and completeness. Three is another favoured number, and here we have religious connotations in the form of the Holy Trinity. Seven is rated the most mysterious of all, due to the seven planets. The Romans and the Greeks rated it the number of good fortune, and it often does well for Aries subjects.

Thirteen however is considered a very unlucky number for dinner parties, referring back to the Last Supper. But, due to the influence of Acora and his Romany convictions, I have found the reputedly unlucky numbers works well for me; so much so that I frequently ask for '13' in raffles and deliberately make important

STROKE OF LUCK ... A black cat is traditionally regarded as a lucky character. Here Prime Minister Winston Churchill strokes 'Blackie', the ship's cat of HMS Prince of Wales *in the summer of 1941: a time when Britain needed every bit of luck in the fight against Hitler.*

engagements for Friday the 13th.

Jeanette, Acora's wife, once told me: 'Like most women I am naturally interested in jewellery and, of course, Romanies have long considered that certain jewels are good luck bringers. Here then, according to age-old Romany lore, are the lucky gems for all the signs of the Zodiac.

'Aries – aquamarine and bloodstone; Taurus – diamond; Gemini – emerald; Cancer – pearl; Leo – ruby; Virgo – peridot; Libra – sapphire; Scorpio – opal (a word of warning here: this is very unlucky for all except Scorpio subjects!); Sagittarius – topaz; Capricorn – turquoise and zircon; Aquarius – garnet; Pisces – amethyst.

'I believe that if you wear or carry something of your lucky jewel, when you've an important date or engagement, influences will usually be in your favour. But, at all times, remember that old Romany saying "Think lucky and you'll be lucky". There's a lot of truth in this.'

That Romany philosophy is profound. Feelings are vital; if we feel lucky, the odds are we'll attract good luck. Indeed the very wearing of say a favoured colour or piece of jewellery probably gives that individual greater confidence. John Grant in *The Directory of Possibilities*, which he edited with Colin Wilson, had this to say: *The supposed power of amulets is thought to reside not in the object itself but in the owner who uses the amulet as a focus for his psychic protective energies.*

The amulet then is basically protection; whereas the talisman's function is not to protect but to *bring* you luck. Your talisman is a personal treasure: a unique object, something special to you or your family. Coins with holes through them, like the old French sou, are considered powerful talismans. Some superstitious people see a coin as a talisman for wealth. They say 'Carry a coin and it will increase your luck.' There are some who, when putting on a new garment for the first time, put a coin in the pocket.

Whether we wear a piece of favoured jewellery or carry some seemingly simple talisman, provided we have faith in that something, our expectation is higher. We feel in charge; our luck seems to move into a higher gear; chance and circumstance appear to be working in our favour and we feel 'on the ball'.

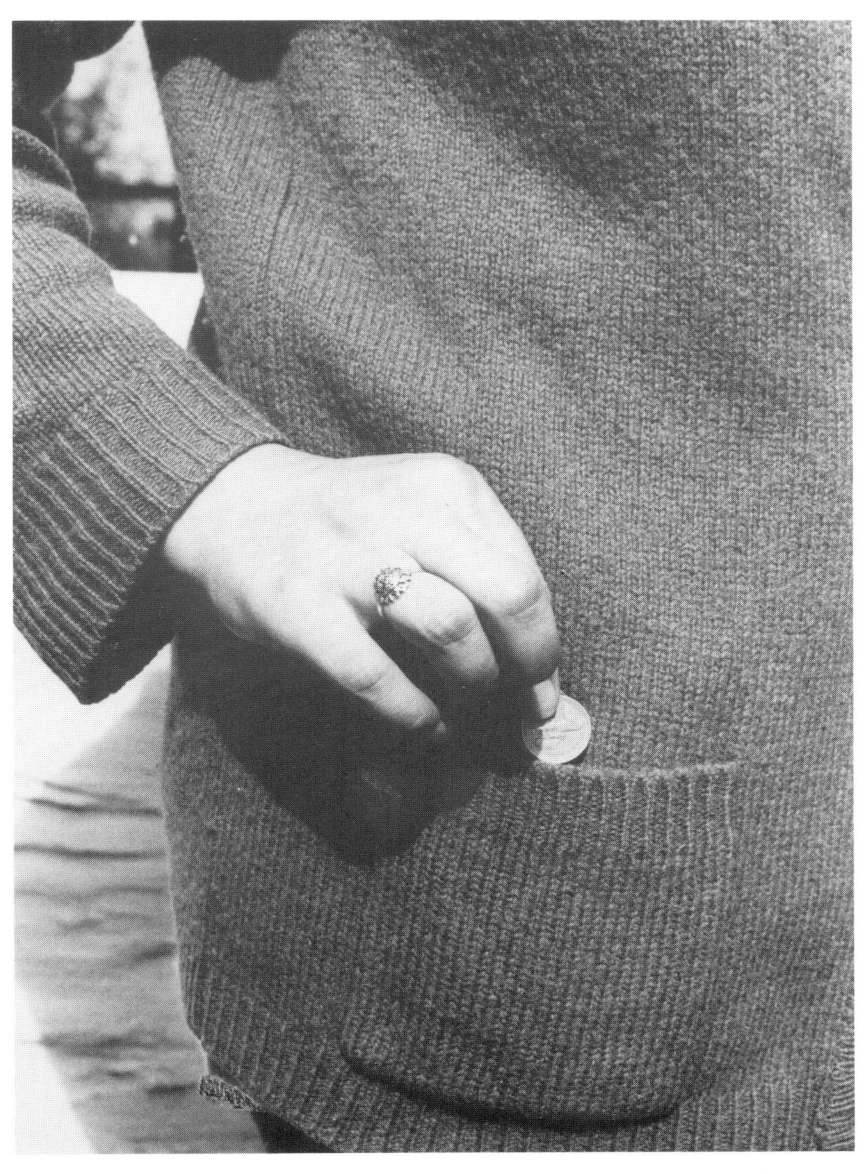

FOR LUCK ... Some people believe a coin is a talisman for wealth – carry a coin and it will increase your luck.

MORE SLIPS IN TIME

THE FLEETING glimpse of a phantom figure may be a flight of imagination or a trick of light. But the sighting of a ghostly building is an altogether more substantial proposition, and we have some spectacular cases in Bossiney territory.

I recently came across such a sighting in Wiltshire. Back in the 1930s Edna Hedges, then a young girl, was riding her bicycle along Ermine Street, a Roman road, just outside Swindon. Suddenly a storm broke and the cyclist was thankful to see a thatched cottage with smoke coming from its chimney. Such was the storm she decided to ask for shelter. We can imagine her delight when an elderly gentleman appeared at the door and beckoned her in. Edna Hedges recalled the man in some detail: he was sturdy and tall, grey-bearded, and was wearing a green waistcoat – but he never said a word. Equally she remembered the character of the building with clarity: dark low-ceilinged rooms and a welcome fire burning. But the curious recollection is: despite the raging storm she heard no noise *inside* the building.

Then, all of a sudden, Edna Hedges found herself back on the road, continuing her journey, and yet she had no recall of making her exit from the cottage. When she arrived at her destination – a friend's house – there were some people present who had just driven up the same road through the same storm. But Edna Hedges was as dry as the proverbial bone. When she told them of her curious experience, she was informed no such place existed on that stretch of Wiltshire road – except for a derelict, unoccupied cottage.

Later she went to see for herself: only the dilapidated cottage

EDNA HEDGES ... who found refuge in a phantom cottage just outside Swindon. Despite the violence of the storm Edna heard no noise inside the building.

and a garden resembling a miniature jungle.

Perhaps not surprisingly, Dartmoor has had cases of, at least, two phantom cottages. Ruth St Leger-Gordon in her book *Witchcraft & Folklore on Dartmoor*, published back in 1973, referred to people seeing such a cottage. Most telling was the experience of an ordnance surveyor who saw a cottage he assumed he had somehow previously missed. From his vantage point, he saw clothes fluttering on the line outside and smoke coming from the chimney, but when he walked in the direction of the moorland property, he found nothing.

Another dramatic account appeared in *The River Dart*, written by Ruth Manning Saunders, published more than forty years ago. Three girls and their father, all strangers to the Moor, went out on a Dartmoor expedition and towards evening the girls got separated from their father and were lost. Suddenly they found a wayside cottage and, as with Edna Hedges in Wiltshire, they gave a very clear description of the cottage: firelight seen through an uncurtained window, an old man and woman crouched over the glowing fire – then, without warning, the whole scene vanished, 'and night, like a black bag, fell over the place.'

Another weird Wiltshire story, deeper back in time, concerns 'a horrible uncouth creature' who had been haunting some woods near Salisbury. On one of his excursions he physically carried off the wife of a local farmer, and only dropped her when he was shot at. He then disappeared. This event was no heightened view of imagination; it was written up and published in *The Illustrated Police News*, March 1877.

How did this 'wild man' suddenly appear in the landscape of Wiltshire? And equally important where did he go?

Charles Fort, who in his lifetime collected a number of wild man reports, believed in the theory – and force – of something called teleportation. Mr Fort reasoned there must be a relationship, as at one end of a tube to another – between locations where characters inexplicably disappear and locations where 'and wild man' turns up. So in each case of a strange appearance, we should look for another of inexplicable *dis*appearance.

Furthermore the Salisbury experience is not unique; in the peri-

FEARSOME SIGHT … 'A horrible uncouth creature' who haunted woods near Salisbury in March 1877.

od 1904-1905 as many as ten 'wild men' were found in different parts of the United Kingdom. One added a new dimension of mystery: he spoke a language nobody understood and carried a book full of writing which made no sense to anybody.

It's an interesting fact though there are more female ghosts than male – interesting because this fact corresponds with the living population. Statistically there are more women in the United Kingdom – and always have been.

Some ghosts are solid, life-like – as real as you or me – but others are less distinct. An especially fascinating case concerned the lady ghost at St Annes, Pittville Circus Road, Cheltenham, Gloucestershire who was seen in and about this particular house for a period of four years from 1882 until 1886. Several people saw her ghostly form, but with the passage of time her figure became less distinct.

I once went into this question of fading ghosts with the well-known Westcountry spiritualist and healer Alan Nance. A man of great sincerity – and modesty – Alan told me he had, on various occasions, talked with people who had 'passed over to the other side' His theory was many ghosts were spirits who were reluctant to leave this world – maybe they loved the place they haunted or perhaps there was some unfinished business; and when they appeared solidly life-like they were demonstrating their determination to stay in this world. Alan further believed when these spirit forms seemed fainter at a later date, this confirmed weakening of that determination, and when a spirit was seen no more, it meant he or she had accepted their movement to 'the other side'. Alan told me he had heard from people 'out there' at seances, and some had said through the medium 'I wish I hadn't put up all that resistance to stay!'

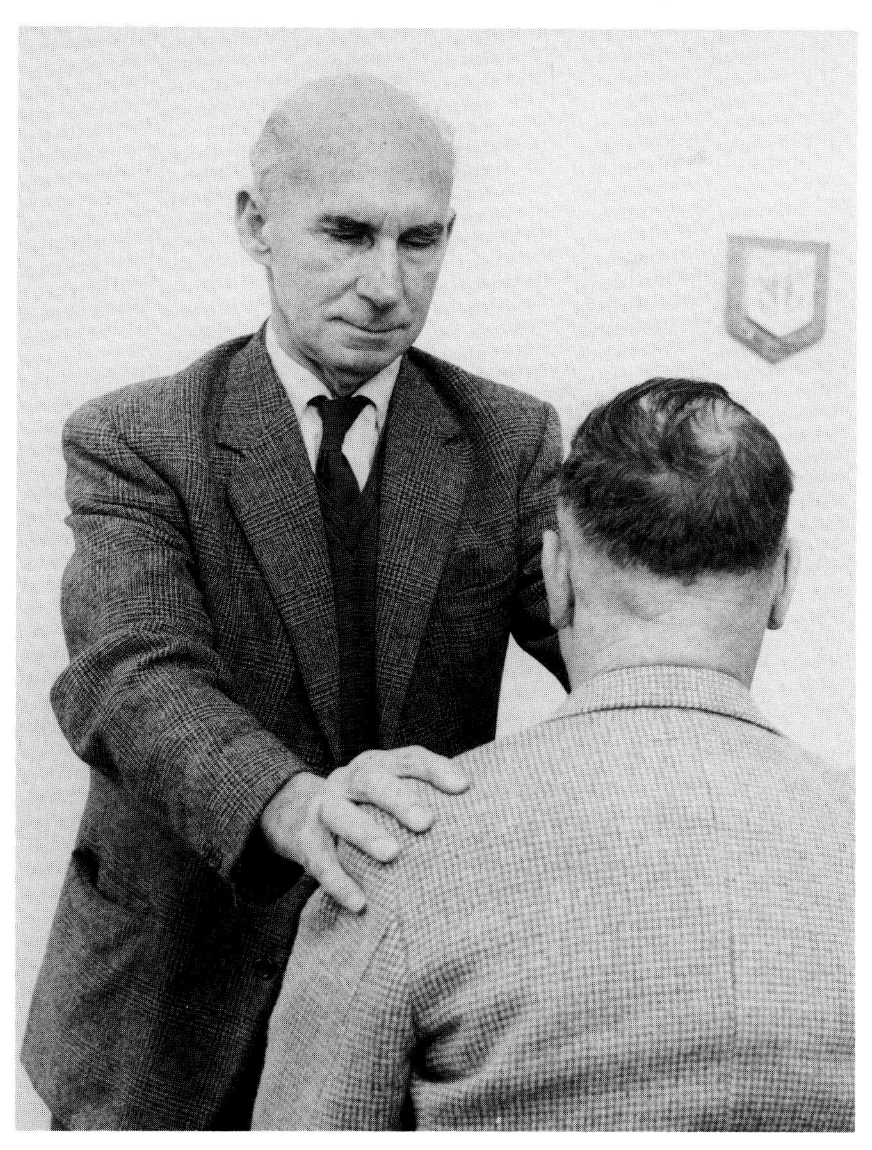

SPIRITUALIST AND HEALER ... Alan Nance works on a patient. Alan was a man who had definite views on people from 'the other side' who came back to this world.

DREAMS

WE SPEND one third of our lives asleep. On average we spend more than twenty years in the realm of the unconscious, that kingdom of our own making where fact and fiction combine to make a curious reality.

In his thoughtful, thought-provoking volume *An Experiment with Time*, Professor Dunne put forward the theory that all the time that is now, has been, or will be, is like a river, and we can navigate this river, forward, backward and sideways, in the vessel of our dreams.

As someone who sleep-walked occasionally as a child and, as an adult who dreams almost every night, I have long been fascinated by dreams.

I have never kept a dream diary, and cannot claim any startlingly psychic dreams, but my wife Sonia will readily confirm in the last fifteen years I have been awakened in the night by the sound of a bell. Sonia assures me no bell has rung on these occasions, but in almost every case that 'dream bell' has been followed by the death of a relation or friend or loved animal – usually within a few days – sometimes within a matter of hours.

It was the supernatural which really deepened my interest in the subject. In 1979 I began researching one of the most remarkable dreams in British history, and it occurred here in Cornwall at Scorrier House near Redruth.

It was experienced by John Williams who had a nightmare quality dream not once but three times on three successive nights. Moreover, each night he dreamed the same dream.

On the first day of May, 1812, he told friends and relations about this recurring dream. Nobody was in any doubt about the location of the dream experience: it was not Cornwall, it was, in vivid detail, the lobby inside the House of Commons. John Williams told the experience in such detail that nobody could fault him. He 'saw' very clearly someone, in a snuff-coloured coat with yellow metal buttons, drawing a pistol and killing a man wearing a blue coat with a white waistcoat.

John Williams had, in fact, dreamt of the only assassination of a British Prime Minister and it took place, precisely as he had seen, in his recurring dream. I have written about it in detail in *Cornish Mysteries*. I mention it here for two reasons: to explain my interest in dreams and to ponder this question. Had John Williams relayed his dream to 10 Downing Street, would Prime Minister Spencer Perceval's life have been saved?

FLOWING ON ... Time is like a river.

John Williams was all for getting a warning message to London, but with wife and friends advised against. They argued it was only a dream and sophisticated people in London might make him a laughing stock.

Cornwall was the subject of another important dream – and murder.

In Wadebridge Churchyard you will find the grave of Nevell Norway – an ancestor of the famous novelist Nevil Shute. He was murdered not far up the road by the Lightfoot brothers, James and William, on his way home from Bodmin Market in February 1840: a crime which aroused enormous public sympathy. Over £3,000 – a considerable sum of money in those days – was raised for his widow and six children.

The crime was to have an incredible supernatural postscript, concerning Edmund Norway, brother of the murdered man. That very night, aboard a merchant ship bound for Cadiz, Edmund dreamt with clarity and accuracy. So vivid was Edmund's dream that waking, he wrote down details, giving a number of important *facts* about his brother's killing. At their trial the Lightfoot brothers confessed they had twice shot at Norway, and twice the pistol had failed to function. They then struck him from the saddle and with several savage blows had killed him – all of which Edmund had seen in his dream. The murderers were hanged at Bodmin Gaol before a large crowd, many of whom had travelled by special railway excursion from Wadebridge.

The fulfilment of some dreams may be attributed to the thing we call 'chance'. But the big question is 'Can they all be a matter of chance?'

Take the case of Mr John Godfrey, later Lord Kilbracken, who had an incredible string of winning dream forecasts about horse races.

In March 1946 John Godfrey dreamt of reading the horse racing results. In the dream two runners, Bindal and Juladin, won races, both at odds of 7-1. On the real racecourse Bindal and Juladin won their respective races, but at different odds from the dream experience. The following month he had another dream and another win. Then in July he dreamt of a telephone conversation with his book-

DREAMER ... John Williams of Scorrier House, near Redruth, Cornwall, who had a nightmare quality dream three nights in succession. The intriguing question is: 'If John Williams had acted on the dreams, would a Prime Minister's life have been saved?'

ATTACK ... The Lightfoot brothers confessed they had struck Nevell Norway with several savage blows.

maker who told him a horse called Monumentor had come home at 5-4. Next morning John Godfrey, not wide awake, consulted the racing page of his morning paper and found a horse with *almost* that name. He promptly backed Mentores and it won at odds of 6-4.

Most serious backers would say the Grand National is usually the

IN MEMORY … The grave of the murdered man Nevell Norway in Wadebridge churchyard. Aged 39, he left behind a widow and six children, and the public collected the sum of £3,500 for them: a remarkable amount of money in 1840.

most difficult race in the year for picking the winner. Well, in 1958 John Godfrey dreamed about a horse called What Man? This time he chose the animal with the nearest name – Mr What – and proceeded to back it. On this occasion, with *almost* the correct name, he had his biggest winnings since becoming a dream backer.

The Irishman's gift – or luck – stayed with him, on and off, for the twelve months and then left him, never to return.

Odd? But perhaps even odder was the experience of Mr John Williams, a Quaker and opponent of all forms of gambling. Before the Derby in 1933 John Williams heard a running radio commentary about the race. But 80 year-old Mr Williams did not hear it on 'the wireless'. He had heard the commentary and the result *in a dream*.

Normally John Williams would not have listened to a Derby commentary – he considered gambling corrupt. However on this occasion, he tuned in to the genuine broadcast. He remembered only two names from his dream: Hyperion and King Salmon. As he listened to the commentator's description of the race on Epsom Downs, he heard his dream all over again – with Hyperion emerging as the winner of the dream and the real race.

The intriguing question here is 'Why did John Williams have that dream?'

At this point in our *Supernatural Investigation* I had a disappointing run – as cricketers would put it – more than thirty people confessed they had never had a dream with prophetic quality. Thirty may not be many to canvass, but the great majority admitted they had difficulty in remembering their dreams.

An especially interesting interviewee was Bossiney colleague Elaine Beckton. A fellow Aquarian, Elaine, who runs her own advertising agency 'Elaine Beckton Advertising' in Cornwall, said 'I've not had a dream for years and years or, put another way, I've not remembered a dream. Maybe I just sleep too deeply!'

Historically though, the Westcountry has had a whole range of prophetic dreams. In the latter part of the 17th century a pageboy was murdered by the butler at Hayne Manor, in the parish of Stowford, West Devon. But for a guest, staying at Hayne, the butler would have got away with it; Mr Weare though saw the butler and his wife burying the corpse under a yew tree. Mr Weare reported the matter to the authorities. The butler was arrested, charged and finally hanged. What makes this an unusual murder case is that Mr Weare *saw the burial in a dream.*

A murder and dream story is also handed down by the Devonshire prophetess Joanna Southcott in the year 1804. A girl deeply disturbed by a vivid dream, called on Joanna's grandmother. The girl, in her dream experience, had walked through fields in the parish of Ottery St Mary. At a stile she met a cat who scratched her breast until she bled to death. The old woman warned the girl never to walk that way again. Ignoring the warning, the girl was soon after found by the stile. She had been raped and murdered. Joanna pointed her accusing finger at the girl's lover. He left Ottery and was never seen again.

There have, of course, been other notable Westcountry dreams. Thomas Grey, a blind man told in a dream to pray at Crediton's Holy Cross Church, did so and was cured. John Trelilie, told in a dream to wash in Madron Well, did just that; he too was cured. The building of Bideford Bridge was ordered through a dream. Milber Church, near Newton Abbot, was designed in a dream – and Bath Abbey was redesigned in a dream.

Perhaps the oddest dream of all was the Westcountry Bishop's wife who, after morning prayers, leading her children to breakfast, told them she had had a very funny dream about a pig in the dining room. While they were all still chuckling, they entered the dining room and found a pig there!

Let the great J.B. Priestley have the last word. In his book *Over The Long High Wall*, published in 1972, he wrote: '*I have no doubt myself that the not unfamiliar déjà vu effect, hinting at past lives, is largely created by the precognitive element in dreams. We have indeed been there before, but it was when we were dreaming.*'

THE HAUNTED THEATRE ROYAL, BATH

THE THEATRE ROYAL, Bristol, is the oldest theatre in Britain in continuous use. It was in Bristol in 1952 that I saw my first professional live theatre: a road to Damascus experience. From that evening I was hooked on actors and actresses – and the theatre. It was thirteen years later I had my first supernatural experience, and some time after that I discovered theatres and ghosts go together naturally – like raspberries and Cornish cream.

Actors, as a breed, are superstitious, and the theatre itself is a place where we are encouraged to suspend 'reality' – where the whole theatre team aims to achieve a kind of magic. Consequently over the years, a solid body of evidence has been built up: a whole range of first-hand accounts, substantiated by actors as well as theatre staff. Indeed a book on all the theatre ghosts in the UK would need to be a very big book.

On this supernatural expedition I made enquiries at my two local theatres: The Theatre Royal at Plymouth, and the Northcott at Exeter. But both times there was a nil return. Neither has had any recorded psychic happening but, of course, both are *young* theatres.

Though I once investigated a curious haunting in a modern council house, on the whole ghosts seem to prefer old buildings. Anyway I decided to do my best to include one theatre with a ghostly reputation and, as a result, I travelled no further than Bath, where the Theatre Royal is one of the most haunted places in the whole city.

A strange sequence of events defying logical explanation have taken place here. In 1963 a clock struck three times during a performance. Nothing odd in that, you may think. But it was distinct-

THEATRE ROYAL … Bath's haunted building.

ly *odd* because the mechanism had been removed beforehand and the hands stood at 12.30!

The ghost who haunts this lovely old theatre is a grey lady. She has no regular pattern and does not always have the same appearance. She appears in an upper circle box, dressed in an evening gown with a feather in her hair, wearing gloves with the scent of jasmine surrounding her. She is sometimes fullbodied; other times slightly hazy, but always totally grey. During 1963 a dancer was rehearsing when he became aware that he was being watched, looking up to the circle he saw the faint outline of a woman.

In 1978 she appeared more substantially and in an active mood. Two young women in the upper circle saw the grey lady sitting close by and she actually turned and waved to them. She has been seen in other parts of the theatre: along the corridors, on staircases, and in the reflection of a mirror.

Who is she?

Some say she was a lady from the 1700s who threw herself from a window when her lover died. Others hint about a complex situation: that she had two lovers who fought a duel and her favoured man died in that duel. A third version is she was a married woman and her husband murdered her lover. Yet another theory is she was an actress who fell in love with a theatre-goer who always sat in the upper circle – but her love was not returned and she hanged herself in the Garrick's Head next door.

Some years ago some interesting facts and figures emerged from a seance conducted by Margaret Royal and the cast for the play *Blithe Spirit.* The messages received at that seance were that her name was Delia, that she died suddenly, probably suicide, at the age of 27 in 1812.

However, seances are not always reliable. So we shall probably never know her identity or the background to her earthly end.

Despite this lack of certain identity the Grey Lady continues to become visible. Her most recent manifestation was during a Saturday matinee of *A Moment of Weakness.* From the stage Liza Goddard and Christopher Timothy noticed a misty figure in the upper circle box on off-prompt side. They went cold and on comparing notes during the interval they found they each remembered the line in the play when they were aware of this mysterious presence.

At this point I am grateful to Jane Tapley, group marketing and

STAGE FRIGHT ... Liza Goddard saw the Grey Lady.

education officer for the theatre, for adding another dimension to the story of the Theatre Royal.

In 1992 she told me: 'In the summer of 1948 Reg Maddox had already written his umpteenth pantomime for the coming season when suddenly he was struck down with a heart attack.

'His son Frank, who was touring with Joyce Grenfell, came to the Theatre's rescue and carried on the Maddox reign, which lasted for almost fifty years.

'The panto which Reg had written was a new version of *Little Red Riding Hood* and included an unusual butterfly ballet sequence. A large wood and gauze model of a butterfly surrounded by lights was to form part of the scene. Frank, assisted by his mother in the costume design, went ahead with his father's plans and became the success of the butterfly scene, the model remained at the Theatre and found a permanent home suspended in the fly tower.

'For the following four years a butterfly appeared either at rehearsals or during a run, and thus began a peculiar association between the Theatre and the elusive tortoiseshell butterfly. Until his retirement in 1979, Frank saw it every year at pantomime and it has often visited in recent years.'

A few years ago a butterfly landed on Leslie Crowther's shoulder when he was starring here in *Aladdin* and another reappeared when Honor Blackman was at a press call prior to her appearing in *Jack and the Beanstalk.*

Even more theatrical appearances occurred during the play *Jeffrey Burnard is Unwell.*

Peter O'Toole, star of the show, speaking to Victor Davis of *The Mail on Sunday* in November 1989, said:

'At the Bath try-out we had an omen, I was on stage pouring a drink when a tortoiseshell butterfly landed on my newspaper. So I ad libbed a chat with it.

'I said, "You are in bad company but you're welcome. Why don't you sit there? But don't make a noise – and don't get pissed."

'The audience fell about. And, when it finally left, I said ta-ta and the audience gave it a lovely exit round.'

There is a theory at the Theatre Royal that a live butterfly at pantomime time, when all good butterflies are hibernating, is a good omen; whereas a dead one is a bad omen. During the run of *Red Riding Hood* a dead butterfly was found outside dressing room six. Two hours later the artist who dressed there was dead.

FAMILY TRADITION ... Omens and deaths have long been linked. Here is Nicholas Kendall, a former High Sheriff of Cornwall, at Pelyn, Lostwithiel, photographed in front of Squire Kendall's portrait hanging in the ballroom. He told me: 'There's a family tradition that when the master of Pelyn is about to die, a phantom coach and pair comes down the drive ...'

EQUINE GHOSTS – AND DORSET

AS A MEMBER of the International League for the Protection of Horses I have a special interest in equine welfare. As a member of the Ghost Club I have a special interest in equine ghosts.

At Rodbourne, Cheney, Wiltshire, a coach and four appear from the past: invariably a bad omen for the family. In Cornwall I have investigated the ghost horse of Ventongimps: invisible hoof beats cutting out suddenly at an ancient bridge. In Devon, Sabine Baring-Gould has written of Lady Howard travelling in her skeleton coach near Tavistock. The Somerset village of Stogumber has the reputation of being haunted by the Wild Hunt: a white horse leading the hunt. People claim to have heard the hunt go through the village in 1960.

Dorset seems particularly strong in equine phantoms: the white donkey of Studland is said to make an annual appearance, about five days before Christmas morning. At Woolbridge Manor a ghostly coach has been seen leaving the house at evening time – something Thomas Hardy used in his *Tess of the D'Urbervilles*. At Trent Manor House there is a hiding place once used by the second King Charles; and a tradition of invisible hoof beats moving along the old highway at night.

The Duke of Monmouth landed at Lyme Regis in the summer of 1685 and there have been various detailed sightings of him riding through the Dorset countryside on a grey horse – again at night.

A string of horses careering through a haunted wood near Blandford – but not a single hoof mark. Two men from the Tudor period leading packhorses on Gold Hill. In the same cobbled area a spectral cavalcade of horsemen, believed to be the funeral cortege of the young King Edward. The sound of horses' hooves and creak of horse-drawn carriages have been heard along quiet country lanes: psychic echoes from the days when the horse, not the motor car, was the principal character on our roads.

Do these equine ghosts mean horses, ponies and donkeys go on to another life? As an animal lover I would like to think so, and I was heartened when an Irish friend, a retired veterinary surgeon, a very down-to-earth countryman recently told me he believed most animals, not just horses, moved on to another form of life after going through the experience we call death.

But Dorset is not only horse country. Dorset is fruitful territory for the ghost hunter in the broadest sense. The county not only boasts many manifestations but an incredible diversity of ghostly character – and characters. The white cow of Whitchurch Canonicorum, a screaming skull, a prehistoric 'Peeping Tom', a

ACROSS THE DOWNS … Not equine ghosts but racehorses in training in Wiltshire. I am inclined to believe the number of ghostly horses seen in the Westcountry and elsewhere is an indication that horses go beyond the thing we call death.

GHOST CLUB ... Chairman Tom Perrot

phantom army and a wide range of mysterious music and noises. These are only some of the subjects. It seems there is scarcely a hamlet without its 'other population'.

'Why has Dorset produced so many different kinds of ghosts?'

I put this question to Tom Perrott, who was born in Bridport but now lives in London. Chairman of the Ghost Club, he is an investigator and lecturer for the Society of Psychical Research.

Here is Tom Perrott's carefully considered reply:

'The more one thinks about it the more one realises how many possible theories might be put forward as a probable answer to this poser. As the question of ghosts is such a nebulous and intangible one, one can only hazard one's only personal theories in the matter, and can only hypothesise as to the reality and nature of their existence.

'Some ghost stories may well date back to the dawn of our history, and could be most likely half-forgotten folk memories of past events which have been handed down verbally from generation to generation. As with the game of Chinese Whispers, the descriptions of these events have often been much embellished in the process of their narration. The telling of ghost stories around the

SECRET COUNTRY ... The countryside of Dorset is full of contrast, and its ghostly population is equally contrasting. There is one manor house in the county with as many as twenty-two reputed ghosts. Dorset provides a whole range of opportunity and challenge for the serious ghost hunter.

fireside was most popular in households, which were remotely situated and 'far from the madding crowd'. Before the days of mass-media entertainment, people had to rely upon their own ability and talents with which to create their own amusements with which to pass away the long winter evenings, an art which now appears to have been, alas, irretrievably lost.

'In company with many other coastal counties, the seaside areas of Dorset were hotbeds of smuggling, and with a coastline consisting of so many secluded bays and hidden inlets, how better could the smugglers protect the storehouses for their contraband, than by widely publicising the fact that many of them were haunted. As a result of the capacious crypts and commodious cellars to be found in many of the churches and manor houses of the country, which were often used for storage purposes, it is not surprising that many establishments of this nature accommodated their own resident ghosts.

'Before the days of standard education, superstition and belief in the supernatural were rife in most of the underdeveloped counties, as was Dorset at that time, and people believing that they were apparently experiencing inexplicable phenomena, would often jump to the conclusion that supernatural agencies were at work rather than make the attempt to find a rational explanation for them.

'Now, as a result of increasing modernisation and development, Dorset people are no less sophisticated than their neighbours in the adjoining counties.

'It is not difficult to see how a century or more ago, a peaceful and largely agricultural county possessing many historical associations, dating back to its very beginning, possessed all the ingredients with which to produce a wide range of ghost stories, which were second to none in the varied history of our islands.

'This does not mean to say that strange and inexplicable events do not occur from time to time, and in so far as their solutions are concerned, one can only put a question mark against them, because we are all aware that there are "more things in heaven and earth" than were ever dreamed of in the immortal Shakespeare's philosophy.'

GHOSTLY CONTRAST

DORSET, as we have just seen, is remarkable in its number of four-legged ghosts and diversity of other manifestations. But I happen to think Cornwall has the biggest ghostly population of the areas we are covering in these investigations.

Some Cornish villages have a number of ghosts; Tintagel, for example, has ghostly monks, ghosts of living people – and there have even been accounts of King Arthur himself appearing among the castle ruins – and some say the ruined castle, now and then, fleetingly reverts back to its former glory.

The Cornish coastline is beautiful but wild and dangerous; not surprising then, there have been reports of ghost ships and cries of shipwrecked sailors. The fishermen and their wives were deeply superstitious – as were the miners.

Cornwall too has a great variety of hauntings: heavy measured footsteps at The Dolphin Inn Penzance, mocking laughter in St Nectan's Glen, invisible coach and horses on the outskirts of St Just, phantom bells in St Ives Bay and high-heeled footsteps in a house in the town, the black dog who suddenly appears and disappears on a stretch of road high above Bossiney – appearances and disappearances which have defied all logical explanation. You cannot go far in Cornwall without encountering such cases.

Across the Tamar Devon, too, is good country for the ghost hunter. I have long held the view that areas strong in atmosphere seem to trigger phenomena. Dartmoor is a vivid example – the moor invariably has an air of mystery and sometimes menace.

A ghostly group of horses and riders, more phantom dogs, horses bolting and throwing their riders perturbed by some unseen threat:

HIDDEN DEPTHS ... The Cornish coastline ... reports of ghost ships and cries of shipwrecked sailors.

Dartmoor is no place for dyed-in-the-wool sceptics. David Farrant, President of the British Psychic and Occult Society, told me of an all-night vigil at Lydford Castle. A trained alsatian dog 'froze' at the top of a wrought-iron staircase leading to the dungeons and repeatedly barked at an invisible something below; and when carried down the stairs the animal cringed in a corner. Later, at precisely ten minutes to three, a dark shape, resembling a bear, materialised in an adjacent room and seemed to glide before disappearing below a stone archway, leaving behind it an icy cold atmosphere. Someone attempted to photograph this fleeting apparition, but the negatives, when later developed, were blank.

In Devon, too, there have been strange happenings in the air. I have interviewed Joan Amos at her Peter Tavy home on the edge of Dartmoor, and she has fat files of sightings: unidentified flying objects, a number of them seen and reported in detail here in the Westcountry. Joan has had several personal sightings, including one over Brentor Church.

Somerset is a county of unfolding discoveries. Only yesterday as I write, a young woman told me of her experiences in a certain Somerset farm house. Despite a carpeted staircase, she often heard a heavy object rolling down a wooden staircase – nothing seen but a good deal of noise.

On a visit to Exmoor in the spring of 1992 a local resident told me, in all sincerity, that a coach and four had had a terrible accident on Porlock Hill – and they have been seen in ghostly form by a number of different people at different times. Porlock Hill must indeed have been a hazardous excursion in coaching days – it's bad enough today in a sophisticated motor vehicle.

Somerset is full of echoes of the past. Many ghosts are unknown characters – simply a man or women from an earlier time with no real identity – but the interesting thing in Somerset is the number of historic figures like St Gilda Badonicus who haunts the Bristol Channel island of Steep Holme and Admiral Howe who haunts

DARTMOOR ... an air of mystery and sometimes menace.

Pulteney Street in Bath. Somerset 'ladies' too have become central personalities in the story of British ghosts: Mrs Leaky at Minehead, Lady Plomley at Locking Manor and there is a female ghost in Taunton whom some say is Maria Anne Fitzherbert, morganatic 'wife' of the fourth King George.

It is interesting in many of our major Westcountry cities and towns, despite development and big populations, we can still get a feel of the past, an impression intensified by old buildings. Bristol is a good example. Bath is another.

Finally on to Wiltshire: back in 1989 I commissioned Peter Underwood to write *Ghosts of Wiltshire*. It arrived on a Saturday morning and was an unputtable-down manuscript. Old houses, inns and churches, even majestic Salisbury Cathedral, and ancient sites like Avebury and Stonehenge, the buildings and the very landscape of Wiltshire seem a natural breeding ground for ghosts.

Then, and again now, I reflect on the fact I'm a lucky man to be living in such a region: such a tapestry of varied paranormal activity.

OLD TEMPLE … Ancient locations like Avebury seem a natural breeding ground for ghosts. Here is 'The Temple at Avebury' depicted on an old postcard.

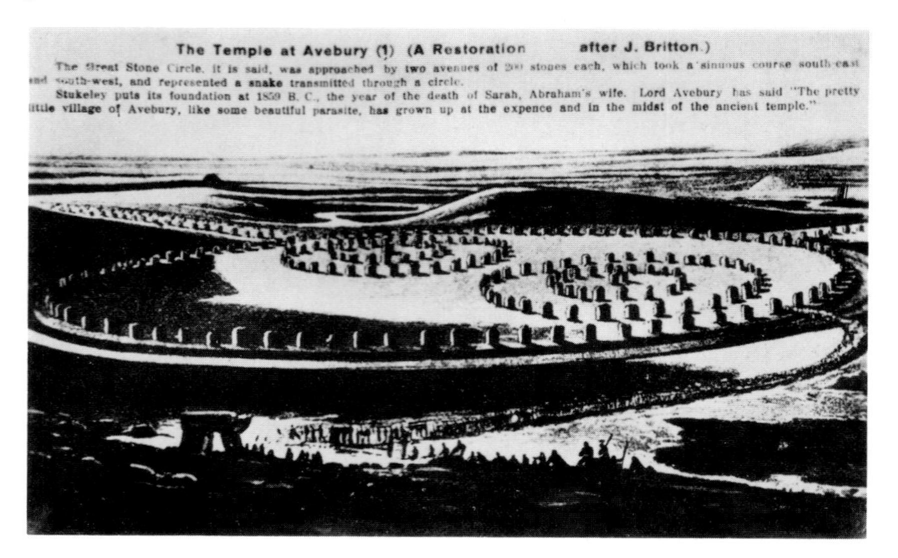

SUPERNATURAL POSTSCRIPT

AS I CAME towards the end of this Supernatural Investigation I resolved to try to give some indication of the range of phenomena.

First though, two thoughts strike: some incredibly fascinating, baffling events have been unearthed, yet there is a realization that a good deal remains secret. For example, I approached somebody about an experience of considerable supernatural significance shared by at least four members of the family: a genuine experience where there could be no question of 'Oh, it was your imagination'. But, sadly, they wanted no publicity for fear of ridicule.

Fortunately some people have no such inhibitions. Only a few days ago in my supernatural files, I came across this *Cornish & Devon Post* cutting from Ida Roberts of Callington, published in September 1982, about a Lifton farmhouse in 1928:

'Fifty-four years ago in the little village where, with my brothers and sisters, we had to walk over two miles to school, and naturally took our dinners, mostly a pasty each, the authorities decided we should have a mug of cocoa hot with our meal.

'As I was one of the eldest it fell to me to fetch a large jug of milk from a small farm nearby, not much more than a thatched cottage really. The elderly widow, or her grown-up son, used to answer the door and I grew to know and like them very much.

'Time passed, and with it came my time for leaving school at 14, with the others of the family continuing.

'One day, the whole village was startled as mysterious things were happening in the little farmhouse, situated near the church on Duntz Hill, strange noises were heard, things in the kitchen and

RESTING PLACE ... Ghosts are incredible in their diversity. They fall into no precise shape or size or clear-cut category. Some are men and women; others are children. Some are spirits from long ago; others are people who have died in recent times. It is therefore logical that many ghosts have been seen in churchyards and cemeteries.

the dairy moved about under their own volition and bits of twig and kidney beans fell on the floor. The farmer's widow, when interviewed, said she had some friends in, and whilst there, 20 or more kidney beans fell about the floor hitting some of the occupants of the room. There were no kidney beans in the room at the time, and how they got there no one knew.

'A young girl working in the farmhouse, helping the occupants, and neighbours at various times, told how the beans came floating along. The son of the house was asked if he thought it was a hoax, but he replied "he was convinced it was not, but they meant to get to the bottom of the mystery as it was causing his mother much worry."

'Some of the villagers treated it as a joke, and laughed about it, while one man said it was, "due to electricity". My own father said it was, "a lot of nonsense," and we were forbidden to go to see the house.

'Rumours spread around the village, and far beyond the West Country. Sir Arthur Conan Doyle was called in, the vicar of the nearby church, was asked to exorcise it, a witch who worked for good, came from Exeter, and saw saucepans with vegetables put on to boil on the stove, but which would be empty right after.

'The poor girl who worked there left under the ordeal, but soon after things became quiet and the spirit or poltergeist, or whatever it was, stopped.

'Good influence prevailed, the occupied had all felt the strain, but things were never really explained.

'Time passed away, as did the occupants, and the old house fell or was knocked down to make room for new houses, but to this day the mystery was never solved, although at the time it caused a great sensation.'

It is a curious fact that some people can see manifestations and others cannot – even when such people are present at the same paranormal happening.

Writing to a Devon paper in 1958, a correspondent recalled a diamond-sharp boyhood memory. In the company of three other people – his parents and his sister – he went to an ancient house on Dartmoor, between Widecombe and Postbridge – where he was menaced by a pack of black hounds. The animals were running loose in the courtyard and the lad was petrified of being bitten – but these ferocious animals were invisible to his mother, father and sister!

There was a sinister happening in Devon during the third week of July 1992 when the church at Buckfast was destroyed in a mysterious fire. The Vicar, the Rev Paul Wilson, at the time of the fire, said: 'We have had problems with Satanic practices but I have no idea who is responsible for this.' At the time of writing, the cause of the fire remains a mystery. It is thought the fire was started deliberately under the altar – but how or why or by whom, all remain unanswered questions.

In the churchyard stands the tomb of the 17th century squire

HELL HOUNDS … He was menaced by black hounds running loose, but his parents and sister saw nothing: a strange Dartmoor manifestation. Stories of ghostly dogs, usually black, abound in Devon in particular – some are said to warn of impending doom, some patrol ancient trackways, some are friendly, accompanying lost or frightened travellers.

John Capel. There is a theory that his hounds inspired Sir Arthur Conan Doyle to write his famous Sherlock Holmes novel *The Hound of the Baskervilles*. Capel was a thoroughly unpleasant character, and there are two versions about his earthly end in 1677. Some say he lay dying while his hounds gathered around his home, howling horribly. Others believe Capel was chased across the moor by his hounds until he dropped dead.

Anyway, local residents feared ghostly reprisals to such an extent they buried him deep in the soil with a mighty stone on his head and a solid altar tomb on top – and to make doubly sure they added a square-shaped house on top of his grave.

An interesting postscript to the whole Capel saga appeared in the *Sunday Independent* on the Sunday following the burning down of the church:

'One villager told the *Sunday Independent* about six men who carried out restoration work at Buckfastleigh's Holy Trinity Church in 1977 for a Capel family reunion.

'Five of the six men died within a few months of each other.

'"Coincidence of course," said the man in a hushed voice as we stood beside Capel's tomb this week.'

I sometimes wonder whether hunches have a supernatural origin.

Winston Churchill, in his heyday as Prime Minister during this nation's darkest hours, backed his hunches. One evening he was entertaining Government ministers to dinner at 10 Downing Street when an air-raid over London began. Winston suddenly left the table and went into the kitchen where he told the butler to put the dinner on the hotplate in the dining room – and ordered everybody in the kitchen to go to the bomb shelter. Three minutes later a bomb fell at the back of No 10, demolishing the kitchen.

On another occasion, after visiting anti-aircraft batteries during a night raid, he went back to his staff car to go home. The near-side door of the car was opened for him because he always sat on that side. Instead he walked round to the other side, opened the far-side door for himself and climbed in. A few minutes later, as the car was driving through the dark streets, a bomb exploded nearby. The blast lifted the vehicle on two wheels, but then righted itself. 'It must have been my beef that pulled it down,' Winston joked.

FOOTSTEPS IN TIME ... There is a strong sense of the past in some of our cities and towns. Path in the grounds of St Mary Redcliffe, Bristol.

GHOSTLY HAUNTS ... It is an interesting fact that some ghosts move along old levels, ignoring alterations in buildings since their death. A good example of this haunting habit is at the former residence of Prince Chula on the edge of Bodmin Moor. The ghost of an old butler climbs the stairs of the Tredethy Country Hotel – as it is now – but he walks on a different level from the existing staircase which was built in 1868. Our photograph shows Rebecca Pickford of BBC Radio Cornwall, right, interviewing proprietress Beryl Graham on the staircase for a radio series we did in 1990.

Later when his wife questioned him about the incident, he said: 'Something said "Stop!" before I reached the car door opened for me.'

Finally, I am indebted to a Bossiney reader in Thomas Hardy's Dorset for a very strange story of prediction. A gentleman by the name of John Snell was curious about his future, and so consulted a clairvoyant. John Snell, then in his 20s, was told he would die in his 44th year. Naturally in his 44th year Mr Snell began to worry – to such an extent that on his birthday he stayed indoors and would not venture into the streets of his home town of Poole! A few days later, in the local paper, he read of the death of John Snell of Poole on his 45th birthday. There had been two John Snells living in the same Dorset town – and the man who had received such a catastrophic prediction, lived to tell the tale.

Here we are at the end of this particular journey.

So what does it all mean?

Some will say 'very little'. Others will declare 'a very great deal'.

That division is inevitable. Men and women have been debating the paranormal for centuries.

The world seems to be travelling through a very difficult, maybe even dangerous chapter. More and more people seem unwilling or unable to climb conventional ladders. Consequently they turn to other means of climbing – like the paranormal.

Many of us are like somebody exploring a strange piece of countryside at night. The torch is doing its job, but we are only seeing so much within the beam of that light.

Now the light of morning is coming, and we are up against some solid wall. If you have travelled with me this far, you may be encouraged to climb up and look over the other side.

PREHISTORIC PAST ... Ancient Wiltshire sites like Avebury and Stonehenge seem to trigger ghostly happenings.

AUTHOR'S ACKNOWLEDGEMENTS

I am deeply indebted to the various people who have told me their experiences in Supernatural Investigation *or offered their considered opinions in answer to specific questions, especially Ray Thomas for his help on dreams. Thanks also to William Collins Sons & Co for allowing me to tell the Plymouth bus ghost story, first publicised in Arthur C Clarke's* World of Strange Powers *in 1985, and to the publishers of two Westcountry newspapers, the* Sunday Independent *and the* Cornish and Devon Post *for the reproduction of stories which first appeared there. For yet another Bossiney title I owe a special debt to Felicity Young and Ray Bishop for their illustrations, Angela Larcombe for her thoughtful editing and last, but not least, Sally Dodd, who, in typing the manuscript made various helpful suggestions.*

Back cover: *Investigating the Devil's Stone at Shebbear, Devon.*

MORE BOSSINEY BOOKS . . .

SUPERNATURAL SEARCH IN CORNWALL

by Michael Williams
Investigates various facets of the paranormal in Cornwall.
'Fascinating reading.' Nancy Hammonds, **Evening Herald**

CURIOUS CORNWALL

by Michael Williams
Words and pictures prove Cornwall has more than her share of things curious.
'... what insights, words of wisdom about Cornwall and the Cornish experience ... not in any forced manner or through any artificial device of compression. I suppose it all arises from a life of interest in and experience of the Cornish scene.'
Dr James Whetter, **The Cornish Banner**

STRANGE STORIES OF CORNWALL

Six writers prove that fact is often stranger than fiction.
'Thought-provoking ... little-known odd occurrences, strange places and eccentric characters.' Adrian Ruck, **Cornish & Devon Post**

GHOSTLY ENCOUNTERS

by Peter Underwood, President of The Ghost Club
Six areas: Cornwall to Wiltshire: a whole range of haunted locations.
'... better read in broad daylight rather than in darkness.'
Frank Ruhrmund, **St Ives Times & Echo**

STRANGE DORSET STORIES

Introduced by David Foot
'This fascinating collection of Dorset tales ...' **Prediction**

MYSTERIES OF THE SOUTH WEST

by Tamsin Thomas of BBC Radio Cornwall
A tour of ancient sites in Cornwall and on Dartmoor.
'There is little doubt that Tamsin Thomas has become the 'Voice of Cornwall'.
Ronnie Hoyle, **North Cornwall Advertiser**

MYSTERIES IN THE CORNISH LANDSCAPE

by Tamsin Thomas of Radio Cornwall
A tour of thirty historic locations in Cornwall by the well-known Cornish broadcaster, starting at Chun Castle down in the Hundred of Penwith and ending at The Hurlers on the eastern edge of Bodmin Moor.
'Tamsin takes us on an enjoyable and speculative canter – literally for she is often on

horseback – through these fascinating and often controversial features of old Kernow.'

Donald Rawe, **Cornish Scene**

'Tamsin has produced a delightful book which will enchant her audience.'

Ronnie Hoyle, **The Western Morning News**

AROUND & ABOUT THE SMUGGLERS' WAYS

by David Mudd

Working through almost forty different sources, including the records of HM Customs & Excise itself, David Mudd (who discovered in the course of his research that his great-grandfather was a Customs officer) has produced a book that is as heady and addictive as the spirits, the wines and the tobaccos that once followed fish, tin and copper as Cornwall's great industries. Several of the sketches and many of the photographs are by David's wife, Diana.

'... scrapes the romantic glitter from Cornwall's erstwhile illicit trade ... Meticulously researched and written in David Mudd's lively factual style it makes absorbing reading.' Alison Poole, **Leader Group of Newspapers**

ABOUT GLASTONBURY

by Polly Lloyd

Here we meet history and rich legend, and in Polly Lloyd we have the perfect guide. The well-known Bristol radio and television presenter takes us on a fascinating tour.

PARANORMAL IN THE WESTCOUNTRY

by Michael Williams

SUPERNATURAL IN SOMERSET

by Rosemary Clinch

SOMERSET MYSTERIES

by Polly Lloyd & Michael Williams

WILTSHIRE MYSTERIES

Introduced by David Foot

CURIOSITIES OF EXMOOR

by Felicity Young

We shall be pleased to send you our catalogue giving full details of our growing list of titles for Cornwall, Devon, Dorset, Somerset, Avon and Wiltshire. If you have difficulty in obtaining our titles, write direct to Bossiney Books, Land's End, St Teath, Bodmin, Cornwall.